Sha[illegible]
Stirred
— BUT NOT —
DETERRED

Shaken Stirred

BUT NOT

DETERRED

Inspiring Stories of Determination, Commitment & Resilience

GLOBAL INFLUENCERS PUBLISHING HOUSE
152 Prince Charles Cr, #17-12 Singapore 159013
Website: www.globalinfluencers.sg
Email: shikha@globalinfluencers.sg
First Published in Singapore by
Global Influencers Publishing House 2022

Title: Shaken, Stirred But Not Deterred - Inspiring Stories of Determination, Commitment and Resilience
ISBN: 978-981-18-5132-2

Printed and bound by Redflame Publishers

Contents

Preface *vii*

Singapore Children's Society *ix*

1. A Run to the Finish Line 1
by Gillian Stapleton

2. Crisis – A Catalyst for Success 13
by Mahal Rajan

3. Crumble & Retreat or Conquer & Rise 25
by Michelle Harris

4. Finding Riches on the Journey of Your Life! 37
by Anita Dadlani

5. Finding the New Me 49
by Dorothy Bach

6. Ibu (Mother in Bahasa) 61
by Rasyidu Samsudin Paddy

7. Learning and Contribution 75
by Nancy Hughes

8. Learning the Art of Saying "No" 87
by Ruchi Parekh

9. Life's Journey to an Unexpected Destination 99
by Elaine Rodrigo

10. Line in the Sand 113
by Omaimaa Mohammad

11. Loss and Awakening 125
by Pallavi Chaturvedi

12. My Choice 137
by Lakshmi Murlidharan

13. Overcoming Barriers to Transform 149
by Nirmala Singhee

14. Rebuilding from the Ashes 161
by Judith O'Callaghan

15. Self Love 173
by Amye Wong

16. The Power of Resilience and Re-Invention 187
by Radhika Unni

17. Walking the Path of a Career Pivot 199
by Valerie Chow

18. What does Life Want from Me? 211
by Patricia Arkenbout

19. What it Means to be Lost 223
by Ghenwa Habbal

20. What Pandemic did to Us 237
by Neera Gupta

Raising Your Voice *251*

Preface

It is a well-worn phrase that "everyone has a story", but not everyone is brave enough to share that story with the world.

Shaken, Stirred but Not Deterred - Inspiring Stories of Determination, Commitment and Resilience is an apt title for this collaborative work of 20 chapters written by women worldwide.

In this volume, we get a glimpse into women's difficulties when their culture demands that they remain subservient, and their need is to be free and contribute to the world.

We learn how to turn problems into opportunities through courage, creativity and resilience.

We travel an author's journey from self-hatred to self-love and the importance of mindfulness in such a difficult journey.

We share another author's journey of transformation that begins with the most difficult of steps – a leap of faith that all will be as it should be. A leap that can and will shake anyone's entire world!

We also learn how the simple act of running can cause the most incredible ripple effects in someone's life - if you remain undeterred by the obstacles placed before you.

Not surprisingly, as we learn to live with COVID-19, there are stories of how the pandemic has changed the thinking and lives of the authors in ways that never would have happened before.

In each of these chapters, the author's life has been shaken and stirred, but their choice has been to remain undeterred and move forward despite the obstacles put before them.

This volume is an eye-opening and inspiring read. Could you and would you be able to achieve all that these women have done? There is much to be learned from each of the chapters and their amazing authors.

Singapore Children's Society

Founded in 1952, the mission of Singapore Children's Society is to bring relief and happiness to children in need. The Society protects and nurtures children and youth of all races and religions.

Singapore Children's Society currently operates 10 service centres, offering services in the four categories of: Vulnerable Children and Youth, Children and Youth Services, Family Services, and Research and Advocacy.

Funds raised through the sale of this volume will support the work of the Society which includes being a voice for our children and their future.

We are grateful for the trust that the authors and publishers of this book have shown in supporting our work. Without their collective voices this book would not exist.

For further information and to support the Society, visit our website at *https://www.childrensociety.org.sg/*

STORY ONE

A Run to the Finish Line

I see the ripple effect of my achievement on those around me.

Emigrating to a new country at 40 and uprooting your husband and two kids is daunting. Years spent assimilating my family into Australian life, building a career, making new friends and learning how to do things the "Aussie way" left little time for me. Then one day, I was stirred into action by an advertisement for a charity that said they would teach me to run if I raised money for cancer research.

Ticking two boxes, 'me' time and appealing to my social conscience, I signed up and showed up. It all started at the sports oval on the coldest Sydney night of the year; I ran a few laps and thought I would die.

Not deterred, I returned the following week with more layers to find other new runners who had also found it challenging but decided it was worth the discomfort. Week by week, we were trained to overcome the fear and breathlessness of running.

A few weeks later, we ran in the Blackmores Running Festival and conquered a 9km run, to be rewarded with a medal put around our necks on the steps of the Sydney Opera House. Feeling like world champions, we had achieved the goal, made lifelong friends and raised thousands of dollars for a great cause. We signed up for our first half marathon – a distance of 21.95km.

That first freezing cold day of learning to run in July 2007, led my friend and I to become great friends, and the two of us to be in Boston in 2013 to run the 117th Boston Marathon.

But first, we went to Paris. Inspired by my brother, who had run the London Marathon to raise money for a mate, my new love of running found me wanting to do just one marathon. My friend and I entered the 2009 Paris Marathon.

We were busy women juggling careers and family life, and we knew running the distance of 42.195km would take a lot of training and time. The added incentive of expensive flights would keep us on track and encourage us to leave the office and complete the 16 weeks of training.

Running my first marathon at the age of 49 around the beautiful city of Paris was meant to be my first and last marathon, but it turned into a much bigger goal.

After Paris came New York, and then undeterred, and with two marathons under my feet, I wanted to complete the World Major Marathon Series, five marathons across three continents, with a special medal at the end of it all.

This series included the Boston Marathon.

The Boston Marathon is an iconic event for runners. In 1967 it was at the Boston Marathon where the first woman officially finished the full marathon, despite a man trying to pull her from the course. At that time, women were not allowed to run this distance. Undeterred and passionate, Katherine Switzer finished the race proving that women could run 42.195km.

The Boston Marathon course starts 42.195km outside the city. Spending the next few hours running from Hopkinton towards the finish line through the suburbs of Boston, the streets are lined with cheering spectators all the way, and college students from Wellesley College encourage runners with signs and cheers that lift your spirits when it gets tough.

We waved to our husbands, who followed our progress. We had 700 metres left to reach the finish line. We were on track for a personal best, and I was on track to complete number four of the marathon series.

Then the road, the view and the scene in front of us changed instantly. A bomb had exploded at the finish line on our perfect day.

The bomb late that afternoon changed so much for so many. People lost limbs and loved ones. Lives were changed forever.

From singing and celebration, all we could hear were helicopters in the air and sirens wailing. Fortunately for us, 700 metres was far from the finish line, and we were not injured.

It simply meant we did not make it to the finish line. We did not complete the 2013 Boston Marathon. We did not get to wear the Boston medal that day.

However, the terror and fear we experienced in those moments were genuine as we tried to find our husbands in the chaos.

Luckily, they were fine. Funnily our husbands have a frustrating tendency to be late for most things and were late to reach the finish line, thankfully nowhere near the explosion.

We walked in the opposite direction of the finish line, trying to decide what next? We were walking away from the finish line we had trained so hard to reach.

My goal to complete the five major marathons was shattered at that minute as we walked, tired, cold and *hangry* (we hadn't eaten for hours).

We walked for what seemed like hours, trying to navigate a way to our husbands. Locals came out of their brownstone houses and offered extension cords to charge phones that were flat so that we could call loved ones. Small gestures that meant so much to us.

I was so cold. It was late on a spring day in Boston, and my body was severely fatigued. The usual finish line space blankets were nowhere to be found.

A woman came out of her home and gave me a black garbage bag. I made a hole in the top and pulled it over my head. It helped keep the body heat in.

Finally, we stopped walking and wearing that garbage bag to keep warm; I sat down on the stoop of a stranger's brownstone house. As I sat there, shaken to the core, lost, and feeling really cold now, I realised that this wasn't the only place in my life where I had lost control over my path and its direction.

As I walked away from this goal that had meant so much to me, I realised it was also time to read the signs and walk away from my job. I turned to my friend and said, "I have to quit my job."

What I thought had been a dream role was toxic, and I knew I could not change it. It was eating away at my soul. It was time to change direction.

In the aftermath of the 2013 Boston Marathon, I was shaken but somehow clearer than ever – I returned home to Sydney and resigned.

It may sound simple, but as the family's breadwinner and in my fifties, I knew I had some challenges ahead. If that wasn't enough, we stirred life up even more and decided to sell the house we had owned for ten years and make a sea change.

Jobless and renting a home, I felt lighter and happier than I had for a while. I could breathe again, and I started to re-focus. Deep down in my heart, the little running voice began again, and I knew I could not give up my running goal. I still wanted that medal.

A worthy goal will always present hurdles, to see how committed you are to achieving it. Training for the Paris Marathon had given me a knee injury, but I had powered through. It was time to find that inner strength again.

Completing the World Major Marathon Series was something I had to do!

The Boston Marathon medal arrived in the mail. Officially, it counted towards the major series, but not in my heart. Those last 700 metres needed to run! I never counted it as number four.

During all this new chaos, with plenty to keep me busy, I entered the lottery for a place later that year in the Chicago Marathon, also part of the series.

Six months on, I completed the Chicago Marathon in my fastest time, returned to a new job, a new chapter of my life, and started looking for a new home. The number four marathon in the series was completed.

Twelve months on from that life-changing day, we were back in Boston. Humbled and privileged to be invited, my friend and I lined up again, 42.195km away from Boston. We stood there waiting with thousands of runners, some of whom had lost limbs the year before. We had returned not to win but to show humanity is stronger than terrorism.

Our mantra: "When the going gets tough, the tough go running".

I have never been so inspired by humanity as I was that weekend. Bostonians welcomed the running community as if they were family, and their spirit returned. So did ours.

In 2014, we completed the 118th Boston Marathon. We crossed the finish line with our husbands cheering us on, and (finally) we got to wear the Boston Marathon medal.

The World Majors were now complete – New York, Berlin, London, Chicago, and Boston.

I have the certificate on my wall.

But in the years it had taken me to complete this goal, the goal posts had changed.

The series now had added a sixth marathon, Tokyo, with a huge medal waiting at the finish line. That little voice in my head returned.

I kept running and completed other marathons, telling myself it didn't matter. It was just a medal. The voice got louder.

The Tokyo Marathon is hard to get into because it is the only one based in Asia. My friend, now busy with a new job, said, "Let's wait and combine it with the Tokyo Olympic year, 2020". My husband, who had supported every marathon to date, said, "Not keen".

There were so many hurdles and so many reasons to let it go. But one day, out of the blue, I called the travel company who did the entries. There were no places left for 2019. Decision made. I was on a waitlist for 2019, or I could run it in 2020. I would wait. More time to train, and I would be turning 60 in 2020—a great way to celebrate.

Weeks later, the call came. My name was at the top of the waitlist for a place in the 2019 Tokyo Marathon. I took a sharp breath, listened to the voice, followed my intuition, and said, "Yes". I would do it alone.

Training on my own was tough. We had moved house again by now, and I had to find new training routes to run, but at 59, in the pouring rain, I crossed the 2019 Tokyo Marathon finish line with my husband cheering me on once again. He had changed his mind, and I finally got to wear that huge World Major Marathon Series medal.

Then I realised it was never about the medal hanging by my bedside.

I'm a better human when I run. It lights me up, and I see the ripple effect on those around me. Other women run now because I run. My children ran the 2017 New York Marathon with me, which will always be one of my most precious memories. A ripple effect I never saw coming. My niece ran a marathon; my accountant took up running, and girlfriends and many more who were watching me now put on running shoes.

Running is my secret to success, happiness, and thriving through menopause; you can find yours. It does not have to be running, but it has to be something you are passionate about, keeps you active and makes you move mountains to achieve. Try a few activities like I did, and you will find your version of running. You must keep moving to keep mentally and physically well. The feeling I get when I head out of the front door, sunscreen or beanie in hand, lifts my spirit and keeps those kilos in check—another great ripple. Meeting up with old friends to watch the sunrise as we run and chat, then grab a coffee, is my therapy.

Try it for yourself.

If you haven't figured it out yet, the medal is a daily reminder that you can jump hurdles and even knock them over when you want to. It is a reminder that passion, determination and focus win over obstacles every time. If moving house, bombs, pandemics and age didn't stop me from achieving my marathon series, I wonder what you can achieve?

About The Author

Gillian Stapleton is a renowned leader and has led multinational global organisations and Australian-based not for profits. An entrepreneur at heart, Gillian has run her own business, served on Boards and is passionate about empowering others, particularly women, to be the best they can be by finding their true passion and thriving.

Gillian has an infectious personality both on stage and in the boardroom. Goal-driven, Gillian has taken many risks in life, not least that of running her first marathon at the age of 49. Since then, she has completed 12 marathons (to date) and is a holder of the World Majors Marathon medal. The ripple effect of running on her life, how she overcame many challenges as a result, and the amazing friendships she has made are what Gill is most proud of.

You can connect with Gillian at:

Email: *gill.stapleton@gmail.com*

LinkedIn: *https://www.linkedin.com/in/gillstapleton/*

STORY TWO

Crisis – A Catalyst for Success

Extraordinary gifts lie within you,
no matter how ordinary you think you are.

I wake up daily, counting my blessings, big and small. I am thankful that I woke up breathing today because I almost did not survive a life-changing ordeal a few years ago. Sometimes, life shifts you from the course you have set for yourself. My philosophy is that through trials, unforeseen circumstances and even drastic changes one may face, we can engineer our hearts and minds to emerge from these as better individuals. That's precisely what I did. I am a stronger version of myself today, and this is my story.

It was around March 2018. I developed a fever that would last for days and then stop suddenly during that period. This went on for a couple of months. Despite running several checks over the months, doctors could not diagnose what was causing this mysterious fever.

Finally, in June 2018, the fever was accompanied by a cold sweat. This was a symptom that I had never experienced. I also experienced migraines that were so severe that even painkillers could not stop them, although they did provide temporary relief.

I knew something was wrong. I was relatively healthy and hardly came down even with the common flu. Wanting to end this, and totally fatigued and weak, I made my way to the emergency ward in June that year.

That was when the doctor on duty ran a blood test which revealed bacteria in my blood. He also ordered the sample to be further tested through a blood culture. This second test revealed the bacteria to be Streptococcus. In my case, it turned out to be a fatal strain. I was immediately admitted and put on 24/7 penicillin drips to flush the bacteria.

However, the recovery process was not as easy as I thought. My highly experienced infectious disease specialist knew there was an infection in my body, and he immediately ran checks on different vital organs. The devastating results showed that the bacteria was in my heart, and I had a rare and fatal condition known as endocarditis, an infection of the heart valve. When my specialist sombrely delivered the news to me, he said the best chance of survival was to undergo heart surgery to remove the bacteria.

I completely broke down. How else does one react in such a circumstance? I thought of my two daughters. They are my world. There was no way they were going to grow up without a mother. I promised myself that I was going to fight and survive. And I did. After successful heart surgery in July 2018, which involved replacing one of my heart valves, I am alive, healthy and whole today.

That incident initiated a new chapter in my life. As I recuperated physically and mentally, I sought answers to questions I had pondered over the years. As I reflected and prayed, I realised that apart from the love and fierce devotion for my family, I was not ready to meet death. My story was simply not ready to end.

One question resonated deeply within me, waiting to be answered. What was my purpose?

Since I was a child, I had always wondered and questioned the existence of life and its meaning and purpose. Why was I born? What was my destiny? My brush with death brought me back to these questions. As I grew up, like most of us, I got so busy with my daily routines and achieving personal goals that I dismissed the more important question. What is my PURPOSE?

I searched for answers from within. I wanted to fight for a cause, use my strengths to help others, and make life better for my family, community and the world. I knew the area and specific group of people I wanted to reach out to – women and youth.

To clarify this, I need to bring you back to the point where this specific aspiration originated. The catalyst behind my venture and book started before my heart diagnosis.

After my daughters were born, my life changed. Being a perfectionist, I strived to be the perfect mother, wife, daughter, and teacher and excel in all the other roles I juggled. I could barely get through the day without feeling drained and overwhelmed. As years passed, without tackling the root cause, the anxiety and constant worrying intensified. Medical research has proven that stress induces low immunity. My immunity was very low during that period.

Many women battle anxiety after becoming mothers for many reasons and are caught between juggling motherhood and their careers. My message to women is simple based on my experience and how I emerged from depression to follow my newly birthed purpose.

You need to take care of yourselves first before tending to others. I advocate that self-care is essential. This simple yet powerful truth can tackle the root causes of worry, stress and depression.

You don't have to wait for a life-changing or life-threatening moment like I had experienced. No matter what stage of life one is at, we need to prioritise self-care. Only when we are recharged can we serve better. Do take time to tend to your physical and mental needs. Self-care can even save your life.

The next area that resonated with me was reaching out to today's youth.

A few years ago, I attended the funeral of a 12-year-old who had died in an accident. At the funeral, I saw her mother. She was watching video footage of her daughter performing. Her mother told me that her daughter would be performing at an upcoming event. It was heart-wrenching, and I wondered why that child did not get to live.

On the other end of the spectrum, there are youths taking their lives. I agree that we cannot understand what someone else is going through. We cannot fully comprehend the grief and trauma of another. However, we can reach out to make a difference.

Individuals grapple with their sense of identity in this digitalised era with unprecedented technological growth and an avalanche of social media platforms. Millions are questioning who they are, what embodies them and what the crux of their identity is. Youths and even adults are constantly bombarded with societal expectations and norms. Is one going to live their life based on the world's definition of what normality is? I believe that identity is an important area to be addressed.

I have always been underweight. I have been ridiculed at school by peers and even adults. Society defines the ideal weight as what celebrities and models embody. I did not fall into the category of being ideal and perfect. I tried to gain weight through various methods, but it didn't work. I simply could not gain weight.

I eventually stopped caring and trying at the age of 25. I stopped chasing after society's standards of normality. I took pride in my values and the person I was within, which surpassed my physical image. I embraced who I was, and I totally love the way I am and look. I am also bold enough to respond politely but firmly when I am criticised about my weight, even today.

As a teenager, I also grappled with my academic and career paths, apart from my appearance. When I was 16, I had to sit for a national examination which would determine which academic path and eventually career path I would pursue. I had absolutely no clue what I wanted to pursue as a career and what I was good at. I could not even identify that languages were my strength and that I should follow those subjects.

Does this resonate with how you were at 16? After some hits and misses, I eventually found my way. But, wouldn't it be simply outstanding if today's youth were more effectively guided in identifying their strengths, talents and areas of interest? There are such strength assessment tools today, but I endeavour to guide youth more closely in the areas of strength, identity and purpose through my training and talks.

If I had found my strengths, talents and passion earlier, I could have channelled the young adult chapter of my life to reaching out and helping the community. I would have had my purpose. I believe that purpose allows you to orchestrate your path towards a higher calling and lead a life of meaning. All of us have gifts, strengths and talents. Wouldn't it be amazing if these were developed and utilised to impact our lives and the lives of others?

If I had found a purpose for living, rather than being buried in the daily routines of life, I could have better managed my emotions in my darkest hours. I may not have been so self-consumed with the role of motherhood and could have had an outlet to channel my frustrations by focusing on a greater purpose.

My search to guide women and youth in the most transformational way made me question what I was good at, and I examined my strengths. I also researched and formulated my model – The Identity Framework.

After two years of training and preparing, I launched my entrepreneurial venture, MetaDestiny, and published my first book, *RePurposed - Finding the New You.* The book guides women and youth to gravitate towards their higher calling using the Identity Framework. The framework comprises the five domains of Self, Decision, Focus, Strength and Purpose. It inspires individuals to prioritise self-care, uncover and tap into their strengths and propel themselves towards their purpose.

To conclude, I would like to share two convictions close to my heart.

Firstly, embrace the moments. You may have heard this before, but do you take time to cherish what's before you? Over recent years, I have learned to slow down and smell the roses, take one day at a time and see the world through the lens of my children.

Children tend to see the world in a way that differs from adults. Have you noticed how naturally curious children are? I recall the time when my kids were toddlers. Have you ever been in a hurry and are desperately trying to drag your toddlers back home while they are stopping to observe everything in their paths?

Pause and observe what our adult eyes tend to miss that catches the attention of the little ones. It might just make you see the world differently. Appreciate life. Let's not look back with regrets. Live, cherish and indulge in the moments. I am glad that I am alive to witness my daughters growing up. Each time I witness a milestone in their lives, they take my breath away, and I stand in awe of God for giving me another chance.

Secondly, never stop striving to be a better you. I have grown to be a better version of myself in recent years. I have ventured out of my comfort zone and propelled myself to new heights, accomplishing things I never dreamed of. Now, I don't believe in perfection. There will always be a better way of doing things. There will always be higher standards to meet in all aspects of life.

I seek solace in trying my best in all I undertake and seek contentment in whatever the results may be. Honestly, I have witnessed that the sky is *not* the limit. So, what's holding you back today? Extraordinary gifts lie within you, no matter how ordinary you think you are. Is there a hidden strength, unexplored talent, or a gift you need to share with the world? The world is waiting for you.

About The Author

Mahal Rajan is a speaker, trainer and author from Singapore. She is the founder of MetaDestiny Pte Ltd. Through her speaking engagements and training, she brings clarity to youths and women who struggle with their sense of identity. Her signature topics are centred on identity, self-care and purpose.

Mahal is a former educator who has served in the Ministry of Education in Singapore for two decades. She holds a Master of Education in English Literature and a Bachelor of Arts in English. As an experienced educator, Mahal also works with other educational organisations in Singapore as a facilitator for various programmes.

Mahal is the author of *RePurposed - Finding the New You*, a book that frees women and youths from their limiting beliefs and inspires and propels them towards their higher calling. Since its launch, copies of her book have also been donated to non-profit women's organisations.

You can connect with Mahal at:

Email: *contact@mahalrajan.com*

Website: *https://mahalrajan.com/*

LinkedIn: *https://www.linkedin.com/in/mahal-rajan/*

STORY THREE

Crumble & Retreat or Conquer & Rise

The one thing you can control is "you" and how you choose to deal with your challenges.

Watching your parents get sick is something you might expect when you're 50, but not when you're 15. When Dad was suddenly rushed to hospital with a brain haemorrhage, this further rocked our already fraught world.

I remember the day it happened clearly. I was in class, and another teacher came in and asked me to pack up my bags and follow him. Feeling worried, he explained that Dad had intense head pains, so the school called an ambulance, and Mum went with him. I was to get my younger brother and sister and go home. Luckily, it wasn't very far as Dad was the school's caretaker, and we lived on the school grounds. Waiting to find out what happened, however, seemed to last forever.

We never expected Dad to fall ill. It was always Mum. With diabetes and crippling arthritis since her early 20s, she was sick for many years and progressively worsened. Since she was always in and out of the hospital for operations, it was something we grew up with.

The weeks and months that followed were very hard. They operated immediately on Dad to stop the haemorrhaging, but he was in intensive care for quite some time. The truth is, this part of what happened is a blur. I did what I always did and suppressed my true feelings. With my world and sense of security deeply shaken, everything felt out of my control. I started to control my emotions by controlling food, which was my way of coping.

Dad eventually came out of intensive care and was in a rehabilitation home for many months, then allowed out at weekends to slowly reintegrate. But he was never the same. He couldn't remember things, and it was like a part of him had gone. It was hard to watch someone you love change and know that there was nothing that could be done about it.

He was eventually deemed fit enough to get back to work. However, he struggled. The appointment of a new school head teacher changed everything, and Dad was asked to leave his job on medical grounds.

Since Dad was the only one working, this added strain on the family, and we received further government benefits to support us. But it didn't stop there. Since our house was tied to Dad's job, we also had to leave our home, shaking our stability further and adding more stress to an already stressful situation. Thankfully, we did get rehoused close to the school.

I decided to defer university for a year after finishing my A-levels and went to work. I was feeling lost and uncertain. It was like all the years before that had backed up, and I was searching for ... something. This was when I started to drink more and found alcohol as another means to help me deal with my feelings.

As a highly sensitive empath, I bottled up a lot and also felt a lot of the emotions of those around me, often taking on the pain of others. I found solace in alcohol, which was also a way to feel released and free.

As Mum and Dad assisted each other (Dad helping Mum physically and Mum helping Dad in mind), plus my siblings and I helped as needed, I resumed my studies and went to College. I was 19.

At the end of my first year, Mum was in the hospital again. I had spoken to Dad on a Saturday night, and he sounded tired. He asked me when I would be back home, as I had just finished my exams and was due to find a work placement for the following year as part of my course.

The next morning on Sunday, Father's Day, my sister arrived at my door. Dad had died in the night of a heart attack. It was instant. In complete shock and overwhelm, I quickly gathered my things and headed back home. Mum discharged herself from the hospital.

The following years continued in more turmoil, with our security and stability further shaken. Mum's health was deteriorating. My brother, sister and I took turns in looking after her so we could each complete our studies and carry on with our lives.

Our home was constantly filled with daily visits from nurses, home helpers and care workers doing what they could to support Mum, so we could all have a relatively "normal" life. But the reality was, it was really hard. Not just dealing with the practical care aspects, it wasn't easy watching someone you love deteriorate in front of you.

Despite the struggles, we still learned and held the values our parents taught us: to show kindness, care, love, loyalty, give a helping hand to those in need, be respectful, be brave in the face of hardship, and not to give up. This is what we did.

One day, sensing the approach of Mum's death, and, as the eldest feeling responsible, I had "the talk" with her about what she wished for after she died. It was one of the most difficult talks of my life. Mum cried, and I cried. But we both knew it was necessary. In her motherly love, she was holding on for us three kids. She needed to know we would be ok.

I was in Oxford, England, when I received the call that Mum had passed. It was seven years after Dad died. She was in hospital at the time and died during the night from a blood clot in her lungs brought on by her other medical conditions.

When I rushed home (just like I had when Dad died), I went straight into "doing" mode. As the eldest child, at age 27, I still felt I needed to be the strong one. We had to leave our house once again, and it was as if life was on repeat with the same stress of not knowing where we would live, but we eventually got re-housed.

When I came to Hong Kong a year after Mum died, everything came crashing in on me. I had felt a deep inner calling to leave the United Kingdom and start a new chapter of my life. However, it ended up a different journey – one within.

I was in depression with deep grief, sadness, anger, and inner turmoil with added fear and uncertainty. I wasn't really eating, and I was drinking heavily; my self-punishment patterns were at an all-time high, and my body was in poor health.

My mind was questioning – "Did I do enough? Should I have done X or Y? What if...." Reflecting on what my life had been like, I had several inner conflicting battles between the need to live one's life and help those you love, the not wanting to be selfish yet honouring oneself and respecting the needs of those helpless and powerless in their situation. I was growing up as a teen yet had to think and be like an adult with responsibilities at a young age. It felt endless.

I began to feel the enormity of the distress and the emotional-mental-psychological impact built up over the years. I always tried to be the "strong one" and bounce back after each setback. The truth was, I felt deeply insecure about myself with a great deal of self-hate. I had no feeling of inner power or a secure foundation of who I was. All of this had been shaken to my core.

In Hong Kong, I was introduced to a local healer, and with energy healing and deep inner work, I started to unravel the pain and heal. I looked at my life from a different perspective: rather than beating myself up and continuing to create feelings of powerlessness, I chose to make a different life for myself.

It's not easy facing yourself and the past. Moving on from the hurt and the regret, the pain and the suffering, it's often easier to blame others or "circumstances". And whilst it may be true that there are things out of your control, sometimes this is precisely what is needed to force us inwards, to our Inner Self, to heal and move forward.

Through this trauma, I learned that despite adversity, the one thing you can control is "you" and how you choose to deal with your challenges.

Compassion is truly known when you feel others suffer. Seeing my parents, as well as feeling my struggle and pain, I developed greater compassion and empathy. I also learned forgiveness and that the most important person to forgive was me.

Having the courage to face myself, I discovered my soul and realised that the feelings of freedom, love, and all I had been searching for for so long weren't about Mum, Dad, or our situation. It was about me.

Feeling insecure about who I was or where I belonged, the challenges opened me to find it within and draw upon inner resilience, strength and leadership. It was guiding me to develop my sense of self and build a new stronger foundation that was stable and secure, based on who I truly was and from owning my true source of power.

My latent healing abilities were revealed as I opened to greater self-love and self-confidence. I went on to create a successful business where I now guide and mentor others worldwide on self-healing, self-discovery and self-empowerment. In strengthening the connection to my soul, I channelled a unique system of healing passed on to me from the spirit that I share internationally. This has encouraged me to trust myself and my intuition as I follow my truth and carve my life path.

We all have our unique soul journeys. Our pain and suffering can be our greatest gift of learning. During my darkest moments, I could have crumbled and retreated. The "dark night of the soul" was at its most intense, and yet, it was life (my soul) that certainly had other plans for me. I took the opportunity to rise – to conquer the inner "dragons" and become a different, more empowered version of myself.

True resilience is not working yourself harder or thinking your way through it. It's also not denying your feelings to just "carry on". True resilience draws upon the pure depth of your soul and inner self. It's facing the challenges of your life despite the adversity, pulling up the deeper repressed "stuff", and having the courage and fearlessness to confront it all with complete openness, awareness and trust. You know you can handle anything when you come out the other side.

Questions for Self-Reflection:

Close your eyes. Focus on the centre of your chest. Take several deep breaths. You might like to imagine sitting with your soul, the inner wise part of you that is always guiding you.

Ask:

- What does my soul wish me to learn in this life?
- What has (the challenge) been about for me? What does my soul want me to learn from this?
- Deep down, why do I find this so challenging?
- How will this challenge help me to grow? What can I do to help myself grow from this?
- Is there anyone I need to forgive to move forward?
- What is the next step?
- Who can help me?

We each can transform our challenges, develop emotional mastery and live a life of happiness. It always starts within.

About The Author

A best-selling author, **Michelle Harris** is the founder of Michelle Harris International and has been guiding women and children to empower themselves for 25 years. A mum, natural counsellor, intuitive energy healing specialist, empowerment mentor and guide, Michelle offers emotional healing, mental health shifts, soul mentoring, energy tools and effective life solutions to those seeking peace, growth and transformation. She is also a channel and the founder of a crystal healing system she developed in 2000 and has pioneered various initiatives in Hong Kong.

A sought-after healer who is well-known for her impactful, deep work to overcome lifelong issues and trauma, Michelle draws upon her inspiring personal journey and shares her discoveries and wisdom in authentic teachings. Her signature individual and group sessions (online and in-person) ignite clients to live their magnificence – personally, spiritually and professionally. Michelle has featured in various media and publications and has received awards in recognition for her work.

You can connect with Michelle at:

Website: *https://www.michelleharrisinternational.com/*

Facebook: *https://www.facebook.com/MichelleHarrisInternational/*

Instagram: *https://www.instagram.com/michelle.harris.international/*

STORY FOUR

Finding Riches on the Journey of Your Life!

The answer was not outside but within.

I am a dreamer, an eternal optimist, and a lover of beauty where everything in life should be perfect. I believe in fairy tales and happily ever after.

I was raised with the simple ambition to be a good wife and a loving mother. I was young, naive, and believed in an ideal world. Life should be simple. I would fall in love, get married, have children and make a home for myself and my family. I would live in my perfect bubble surrounded by the people I love, doing things that made me and those around me happy for eternity.

However, my destiny had a different plan. It designed an adventure instead, a rollercoaster ride filled with twists and turns, highs and lows, featuring tests and challenges, heartaches and joy, resulting in rich experiences.

My amazing journey started when I was young and fell in love. I discovered that alcohol and addiction are bad for relationships. This led to divorce, and soon I learned about independence and understanding what it was like to live from paycheck to paycheck.

Then I found love, a love so beautiful, tender, and absolute that I was filled with a sense of wonder that such love could exist. I felt blessed that life had given me a gift when I met my soulmate.

My partner and I relocated, and I adapted to a new lifestyle and reinvented myself. Around that time, my mother passed away. It was all so sudden.

I was left to pick up the pieces and nurture my father with his fragile heart. I had to shuttle between two cities, so I learned how to balance my partner and father, who both needed me physically and emotionally.

I witnessed criminal business practices and had to work twice as hard to support my household financially. These were all significant turning points in my life journey. At every juncture, I only got richer internally. I always found a way to get back up on my feet. I had faith that I had the strength and courage to do what I had to do.

I didn't expect anything in life could get worse, but it did.

A few months later, my father passed away, and I was still reeling from the blow when my maternal uncle, as close to me as my dad, passed away.

But that wasn't the end of it.

I faced one of the most challenging moments of my life. It was a turbulent time. I use the word turbulence to express the intensity of the situation. I lost hope in the chaos. I felt ripped apart.

It was Sunday morning, 21 July 2019. I was relaxing with my partner in our TV room. I caught a whiff of something burning. Despite the cool air from the open window, I could feel a lot of heat.

I opened the door and was shocked to see a fire blazing in the corner of our living room. It was crackling and sputtering flames. I called out to my partner that there was a fire, and my first instinct was to get help.

I dashed out barefoot, rang the neighbour's doorbell and shouted, "Fire". Neighbours arrived with fire extinguishers. They suggested that I go downstairs while they tried to stop the fire.

Knowing my partner, I knew he would try to help them. As I ran down three floors, the fire alarm was triggered. I was rushed out of the building along with the other residents. What followed was a frantic blur.

Standing outside the building in the crowd, watching our building being consumed by the raging fire, I looked around but couldn't find my partner. My eyes were burning from the smoke. I felt sick to my stomach.

I remember shouting and screaming my partner's name. I was yelling my lungs out. I couldn't see him anywhere. I ran to the other side of the building, calling repeatedly.

My heart was pounding, and my throat was clogged. People kept asking me what had happened and all I could say was that he was missing and to please find him. I remember repeating to the firefighters that he was missing, that he must be unconscious somewhere inside the flat, and that they needed to help him.

I tried to run inside, but they held me back. It is impossible to express how I stood there, feeling the intense heat, listening to the glass shatter and watching thick black smoke escaping through the windows.

The firefighters brought someone out. I felt a sense of hope that it was my partner. It was not him. I begged the firefighters to look for him.

"We have cleared the building. There is no one inside," they said. And yet I knew, deep inside, something did not feel right. After an eternity, they found him, brought him out, and put him into an ambulance. They wouldn't let me ride with him. It was an emergency case. When I arrived at the hospital, they told me he was no more.

At that moment, my world shattered. My heart felt like it had been burnt in that fire with him.

This time, I couldn't recover. Something inside me broke and hurt my spirit. Three deaths in a row. My partner – the love of my life, my soulmate, my best friend – was gone.

We were a team – two parts that made a whole, my Prince Charming and my hope for a happily ever after. I felt like someone had cut off a piece of me – I was incomplete.

I had nothing of the life we had built together. . The fire destroyed everything: my home, belongings, and my beloved. What was once a happy place was now just charred black debris.

It has now been exactly three years since this tragedy occurred. The world has been hit by the pandemic since then. People's lives have changed.

As I look back and reflect on all the curveballs life threw at me, I can only say that my life has only become richer. And, you may wonder why.

It is because I met two new friends, Grief and Trauma. Since I was so tired, they took over my life journey for a while. Both were strong, taking me to dark and lonely places, losing me in sadness and emotion, dragging me down so deep, keeping me locked away from my spirit, and making me lose the will to live.

But when life is built on a foundation of hope and faith, the light finds the strength to shine again. I cried for help and recognised that asking for help was not a sign of weakness but strength. I was going to try to live again. Grief and Trauma still surround me, and I often try to fight for the wheel in the driver's seat, but I am stronger than that!

Now I understand them and have learned their sneaky ways. I know how to manage their triggers and understand what I need to do and how to deal with them.

Grief will never leave. It is here to stay with me, but we are finding ways to live together as time progresses. I find Grief a place that is not so overwhelming and does not linger for too long.

Another friend is Love, a very significant player on my journey. Despite the pain, Love ensured family and friends always surrounded me. I have had an abundance of love sent my way.

Love has been there, taking charge of my life, giving me a home and a safe space, helping me to heal, and allowing me time and space to mend without pressure or influence. Family is priceless and unconditional. Love brought children into my life, reminding me how simple life can be, where we have no burdens and stress of day-to-day living, just waking up, playing, eating and sleeping – teaching me how to smile from within again.

Love has shown up for me in so many ways – shining on me externally and internally – it has taught me to love myself. I know what I need, how I feel, and how to care for myself. Love has helped me strengthen my relationship with my spirit to survive. I am letting go of things that don't serve me and holding on to what I need to grow and bloom.

I cannot forget my friend Gratitude – who was there before but was pushed aside by Trauma and Grief. Gratitude guides me to appreciate the small things and changes my perspective by assuring me that no matter what the situation, something good will come out of it. This helps me refocus on achieving a comforting mindset, giving me time to pause, reflect and appreciate the abundance that continues to flow my way daily. By adopting an attitude of gratitude, I will manifest a more meaningful life.

Lastly, my trusted Faith has been there constantly. In all the years of my life, our bond has only become more robust. In these last three years, I have held on to Faith as tightly as possible.

The power of Grief and Trauma were strong, and they tried to push Faith out of the way, but because I have such a strong connection with Faith, their collective power was no match when it came to Faith.

Faith showed me how to clear the way, finding the first step to start climbing up again, even though the way was dark and the path unknown. Faith held me close, and we took each step together. Fear and Anxiety have joined us occasionally, but Faith ultimately keeps walking by my side.

Time heals everything, and it rings true here too. I have reflected on my rollercoaster journey. There have been many achievements in the professional and personal space, and now this incredible opportunity to start over, reset and restart. This has given way to new possibilities and new beginnings to make my life rich again.

With my supportive family and friends, I have the proper foundation. What can I do to make life even richer?

I looked around, inquired, read and realised the answer was not outside but within. So I started questioning internally to reconnect with my spirit.

What is my purpose? What am I doing here? And as the darkness started to clear, I could hear it again, I could feel again, and I heard it say, "Your light – shine your light. Reach out and spread love and happiness all around you." At that moment, I felt a spark, it was my truth, and it felt right.

The time has come to grip the reins of my life and retake charge. This time, it will be to shine my light bright, wrapping as many as I can with happiness and kindness, sharing my stories and life experiences. I will introduce my friends, Love, Gratitude and Faith, sharing the tools one needs to live a more fulfilling and enriched life.

As I conclude, I ask you to take a moment, close your eyes, look within and ask yourself, "Can I shine my light? Can I make this world a better place? Can I contribute to myself, my loved ones, and those I associate with? Can I share and contribute to spreading happiness and joy?"

As life flows on its course, we will face unnerving moments. This is a test. Know that you must continue to flow and do what you need to survive. Also, ask yourself how you can enrich your life to become emotionally richer.

Everything you do, every experience, every person you meet, and every place you go will help you to grow. Make sure you take Love, Faith and Gratitude with you, and they will ensure that you get to experience the magnificence of your life journey.

As I fill my life account with wealth, I wish you the same. Shine your light and enjoy your ride on the journey of life!

"We shall never know all the good that
a simple smile can do."

—Mother Teresa

About The Author

Anita Dadlani is an entrepreneur and recognised professional in the PR and Events Industry.

She has successfully managed the public relations of leading brands and business across a range of industry segments in Hong Kong, Dubai and India.

With over 25 years of experience, Anita is passionate about working with businesses and entrepreneurs to help design their brand stories. She works with them to understand their goals and designs solutions to create maximum impact. She firmly advocates that you are your best PR.

She has an extroverted personality and enjoys meeting people and learning about diversity and culture. Her network and reach have developed into a new agenda of building communities based on the foundation of happiness, positivity and collaboration.

You can connect with Anita at:

Email: *poojaanita@gmail.com*

LinkedIn: *https://www.linkedin.com/in/poojaanitadadlani/*

Facebook: *https://www.facebook.com/poojaanita*

STORY FIVE

Finding the New Me

We are all stronger than we think we are.

Panic

"Mama, help me! I don't want to die!" my eleven-year-old son pleaded, locking his panic-filled eyes with mine.

His mother was the only person he knew who would keep him safe. She could save him. She was always there. She always knew what to do. She always found a way, except for this time. I didn't know what to do to save my own life. But I am his mother. I should know.

"Please, I can't do this. I caaan't..." His fingers were clawing at my shirt like a tiger who caught his prey, ready to tear the skin off his meal. His eyes looked so distant, like the bottom of the well.

"Help him! For goodness sake, do something! Just anything! Don't just stand there, you fool," my mind was screaming at me at a thousand decibels while watching my son helplessly clinging onto me for dear life.

People in the mall lobby watched the circus unfolding in front of them, staring at the delirious boy and his useless mother, who was doing nothing except cradling him in her arms and saying, "The car will be here soon," over and over again. I could feel disgusted stares burning right through me. "What kind of mother is that? Why isn't she doing anything?"

Half an hour into his anxiety attack, my son was curled up on the bench in the fetal position, his breathing shallow and fast, as if he had just run the New York Marathon with his little legs having given way under him.

An hour ago, we had come from his psychiatrist, where he was diagnosed with depression and general anxiety disorder.

We were going to buy his new medication on the way home after the mall when he experienced his very first anxiety attack – our first anxiety attack. Nobody, absolutely nobody, was prepared for what had just happened.

Betrayal

I took my marriage vows to heart, "…to have and to hold from this day forward, for better or for worse, for richer, for poorer, in sickness and in health, to love and to cherish, until death do us part."

I threw myself into the marriage. I loved this man and believed we would be together forever. I honestly thought we could conquer all that would come our way. However, at some point, I saw cracks in our marriage, and we started leading what seemed like parallel lives.

I guessed that with all marriages, daily life and challenges could take over after over twenty years together. They say you will have flashbacks of your past when you are dying, like in most movies. When I was dying, my flashbacks went all the way to fifteen or twenty years earlier, when

I suggested to my husband, "Let's go for marriage counselling," and his response was a simple, "No. I don't want to."

I was wrong about always being able to fix things. I thought if each partner puts 50% into a relationship, then that couple should do just fine. I learned later in life that was not true. Each person should put 100% into the relationship. We have to put in the work. We have to put in the effort.

When I was nineteen, a very dear loved one told me that a relationship needs to be tended to. It does not matter what type of relationship – family, friends, business or your romantic partner – needs to be nurtured. A relationship needs constant care and nurturing like a flower needs sun, water, fertiliser, and even kind words. It requires a gentle touch. Once you stop, the flower wilts or even dies.

I carried these wise words with me throughout my life. It made so much sense to me. And I saw firsthand from this particular loved one what an amazing relationship and marriage they had. They were rock solid and bulletproof. Even after decades together, they were still deeply in love, holding hands, and I would even catch them gazing lovingly into each other's eyes. I wanted all of that.

"I want to push you in that wheelchair when we're old, even push you down that hill and let go," my husband and I would joke and laugh together. "I want to sit on that bench with you when we're all wrinkly."

I was so in love with this man. We were so in love with each other. He was my rock, my best friend, my lover, my life, my heart and my soul. I was looking forward to old age.

Unfortunately, my husband's behaviour started to change. My world turned black when I discovered his heart laid somewhere else. I was plunged into depths I didn't even know existed. My heart was ripped into a thousand pieces. I couldn't breathe.

I thought we were rock-solid just to discover we were mere mortal beings. Twenty-two years together and being married for eighteen years did not make us invincible. "Help me!" I screamed into my head, into the void. "No, I can't do this," I tried to cling to life. "I want to die!"

I begged the Universe to save me. I was like my son when he was having an anxiety attack, but the only difference was I had nobody to save me, to hold me, and to give me words of comfort. I was all on my own when my world came crashing down.

Triage

My husband and I had a trial separation in the hope of clearing out things in our hearts and minds. It was a challenging and painful decision, but I so desperately wanted to save us that I chose to do the very thing that scared me the most – letting go in the hope that we'd find our way back to each other again, whole.

I ran a triage at home, trying to hold everyone above water. But in all that saving, I forgot about myself. I was numb and just kept going because I had no choice. After all, I am a mother and a wife. Isn't this what we're supposed to do?

I was in disbelief when my husband told me, "But you're so much better at this than I am." I wondered if it was a fair argument. I knew I was a strong individual, but even strong people have their breaking point. But did I have any choice other than to throw myself into the family and kids even more than I did before?

None. I realised I needed to do the saving because I was "better" at this than he was. So I poured myself into the family because my kids needed me now more than ever.

About a month after we started the trial separation, I was sitting hunched next to my son, who sat on his bed, vomiting and shaking, as he had one of his anxiety attacks. I held him with one hand while my other held a little toy bucket I managed to grab and hold under him as he was throwing up.

On the other side of the room, my five-year-old daughter was wide-eyed with fear, grasping her blanket and watching her brother lose himself to this beast that consumed him. I could see this fragile little girl needing her mama to hold her and tell her everything would be okay as she was too young to understand any of what was happening.

I hated my husband so much at that very second. I was there, having to deal with the situation alone instead of both of us together. I hated how I had to choose one child. I was made to choose, and that killed me. How do you choose one child over the other?

I held my son while looking at my daughter. Hot tears burned holes in me, and my throat tightened so that I could barely breathe. It was like someone was squeezing the last bit of life out of me.

Depression and Exhaustion

I gave my all as a mother and wife as I forgot myself in the process. There was nothing left of me. I was numb, empty, and hurting. I was exhausted mentally, emotionally and physically. I had finally run out of steam and crawled on all fours.

I was still crawling because I had to keep going for my kids, who depended on me. It was not even a choice for me to give up or lock myself in the room and never come out. That would have been so much easier. Who knows if I had chosen the easier way of giving up and giving in? What would've happened to us?

Trying to be the best I could as a mother to my kids suffering from our situation and who were not well and holding my head up as a blindsided wife, I suffered PTSD. The betrayal was the hardest part for me to process.

The day I was diagnosed with depression, it made sense to me why I was an emotional wreck from the moment

I discovered the infidelity and the three-year affair that followed when he left us.

New Beginnings

It was a rollercoaster ride trying to save my son who was sick, my daughter who was getting sick, my marriage that broke down, and finally, myself, who fell apart. It was not easy to let go of twenty-six years when that was all I knew. I would have never believed it if someone told me that motherhood and marriage would change my life forever.

This was certainly not how I imagined it to be. My path towards the end of the marriage was painful and lonely. And although there were times that I felt I couldn't do it, I just put one foot in front of the other.

We have to trust the process. We are all stronger than we think we are. We have it in us. We must have faith, be patient, and hold on to hope. I discovered we should not underestimate how the right kind of support and help can lead us to a path of healing.

Cry it out on your friend's shoulder or over the phone, receive a warm embrace or a gentle touch, seek professional help, and take medication if that's what you need. Read, watch, educate yourself, change your perspective, make yourself look pretty for no one but yourself, have a massage, workout, take up a new sport, meet new people, go out . . . you name it. Do what feels right for yourself. Just do not stand still and let life consume you.

Although I felt like I was the only person going through this at the time, I discovered that I wasn't. When I started showing vulnerability, many women reached out to me who had similar painful stories to share. Many people hide their pain as I did. Maybe I had to die to be reborn and be where I am today.

If I could let one person who is hurting today know that they will be okay, this painful journey would've already been worth it.

At forty-nine years old with two young children, I am a single mom starting over after going through my darkest hours. I am not afraid to tell my story and am proud of myself for not just putting myself back together again but doing so in less than a year.

I am finally happy, and I feel more alive than ever. I know my kids will be okay, too, because I chose to put on that oxygen mask in the plane before putting on theirs when I was crashing. When I decided to look after myself better, I could be a better mother to my kids.

My life is only beginning, and I am excited about what the future has in store for me.

About The Author

Dorothy Bach is half-German and half-Filipino. She was born in Bangkok and has lived in Indonesia, Germany, and the UK.

Manila has been her home since 2010 with her extraordinary son and daughter, five rescued cats, an adopted puppy, and piles of books.

Dorothy studied at the European Business School London (EBS London) with a semester at the European Business School Madrid (EBS Madrid) completing a Bachelor's Degree in International Business Administration.

She took time off work when she became a mother to focus on raising her children.

She is a very passionate mental health, gifted, and special needs advocate.

As a child, you would often find Dorothy pouring over books in the library. The love for reading was instilled in her at a very young age by her parents who were walking libraries. Writing has been a natural next step.

You can connect with Dorothy at:

Email: *dorothybachwrites@gmail.com*

LinkedIn: *https://www.linkedin.com/in/dorothy-bach-a914a0248/*

Instagram: *https://www.instagram.com/dvanmiert/*

STORY SIX

Ibu (Mother in Bahasa)

When you hit rock bottom, the only way to go is up.

I lost my mother when I was 18. Her death was not when I hit rock bottom. Finding out about her diagnosis was.

My story began on Friday, 6 April 2007. It was Good Friday that year.

I was out having lunch with a couple of schoolmates from junior college. We had just received the results of our GCE 'A' Levels. The three of us were spending the afternoon discussing our future aspirations.

Somewhere at the back of my mind were thoughts of my mother. My sister had arranged for our mother to be seen by a traditional healer since she'd complained about a numb feeling in her legs in the past few weeks. I recalled how my mother started limping and relied on an umbrella as a walking stick.

We were almost done with our meal when I received a phone call from my sister.

"Ibu vomited at lunch just now. We're sending her to the hospital," said my sister, referring to our mother, as they rushed to the hospital's Emergency Department.

I left my friends to meet my family at the hospital.

~ ~ ~

I entered the hospital's Emergency Department and found my mother in the triage area. She was being attended to by a doctor assessing her symptoms. At that moment, my mother described that she had been experiencing a recurring migraine for months that was not going away despite her best efforts at self-medicating.

The doctor checked her eyes and took down some notes, all while looking quite concerned.

"We'll have to admit her and do several tests. Her symptoms seem consistent with that of stroke," said the doctor.

It took a couple of hours before the hospital finally found a bed in the ward for my mother. As my sister sorted the paperwork to get our mother admitted, the nurse on duty approached me.

"The doctors have ordered a CT scan and MRI for your mother tomorrow morning. We'll need your agreement by signing these documents."

After speaking to her, a doctor walked to me and asked, "Did your mother ever tell you about the lump in her left breast?"

I was in a daze. I recall my mother casually mentioning her discovery of a lump in her breast a few months prior. It was information I had no clue what to do about. I remembered my much older sister asking her to get it checked, but neither of us knew if our mother had taken any action.

I left the hospital that evening to return home with my father, feeling a whirlwind of emotions – tired, confused, and anxious. It was not a very good Friday, as it turned out.

Ibu (Mother) had her CT scan and MRI the following morning. I received a call from the hospital sometime that day, with the doctor requesting to see the whole family at the hospital. It was a weekend, and the fact that the doctors had asked to see the family on that day seemed urgent.

My sister, father and I hurried to the hospital, where we were directed to an available meeting room in my mother's ward. As it was a weekend, my mother's sisters had made it to the ward to visit her. We let them be with my mother as the three of us were ushered into the room.

We were seated opposite a panel of three doctors about to reveal their findings. I was mentally prepared for them to say that my mother had suffered a stroke caused by a blood clot in her brain. Her father suffered from the same condition, and after the doctor's remarks in the Emergency Department triage area, I was mentally ready for this news.

"Is this all the immediate family members?" one of the doctors asked.

"My brother is overseas. I will update him right after this," my sister replied. My brother worked in the army and had just been deployed to an overseas camp on a year-long assignment.

"All right," the head doctor began, taking a deep breath before continuing. "We wish to assure you that our doctors and nurses are here to support your family in this trying time."

He paused.

"We conducted analyses of your mother's CT and MRI this morning. In light of her feedback about the lump in her breast, we had also ordered some tests to determine what it is."

"We're sorry to share that your mother is diagnosed with stage 4 breast cancer, and cancer has unfortunately metastasised to her brain. A secondary tumour in her brain is impacting her mobility."

I was listening intently, but there is only so much one can process at that moment. The closest I'd come to the words "cancer" and "tumour" was in a television drama series. Never had I imagined encountering it within my own family.

My father was already having difficulty breathing as he took in the news. Just a month before, he was diagnosed with Chronic Obstructive Pulmonary Disease (COPD) – a chronic lung condition resulting from his long-term smoking.

"So, what are the treatment options, doctor?" my sister asked, fighting back the tears.

"Unfortunately, as it is already in its last stage, few options are available. We can, however, still remove the tumours to try and stop the spread of cancer to other parts of her body."

"Will that help increase her chances of survival?" I eagerly asked.

"If you do not remove her tumours, she will have one to three months to live. Removing the tumours may prolong her life by a few more months – around nine to 12 months."

"Okay. But…?" I queried, waiting for them to present any possible downsides from offering the solution.

"But removing the tumour in her brain will be a very complex surgery. There is a risk of paralysis, and she may be bedridden after that for the rest of the time she has left. Or she may not even survive the operation," said one of the doctors.

I felt my world crashing down at that moment. I was struggling to internalise everything that I had just heard. The words were spinning in my head.

Our family decided to let our mother proceed with a mastectomy, though we decided against the brain surgery as we did not want to take the risk. As I was in a life transition, waiting to enrol in university and only working a temporary job for some extra pocket money, my sister and I agreed that it was best for me to quit my job to care for our mother during whatever time she had left.

The next few weeks and months were about providing the best care for my mother. After the surgery to remove her breast, I saw how my mother was still determined to keep it all together and not rely too much on others for help.

She had tubes hanging from the part of her chest that was removed and had to carry around bottles draining the blood from the operated area, which made it a challenge for her to get on with her daily activities, though she battled on.

My mother remained strong, but there was no denying the reality that she was no longer her usual self. From where I stood, I could see how having her breast removed and realising her mortality affected her sense of self.

I went through the different stages of grief, from shock to denial and even being angry at myself sometimes. I continued questioning myself, asking why I had not insisted on taking my mother for a mammogram when she first mentioned the lump in her breast.

On 12 May 2007, my sister gave birth to her daughter. I took my parents to the hospital to meet their first grandchild. My mother's mobility was severely limited by then, and we had to push her around in a wheelchair.

I remember very clearly when my sister asked if my mother wanted to cradle her baby. I could see in my mother's eyes her desire to, though she was a little hesitant as she looked down at her hands, noting how weak she had become. Her sister, who was also present, offered support as my mother extended her arm to receive the baby.

The sight of that was too much to bear. It was a paradoxical, poignant moment of pure joy wrapped around a heartbreaking situation. I held my tears back as I walked out of the room and later broke down alone in the corridors of the hospital ward.

My older cousin, who saw me from a distance, approached me and hugged me. She said, "You need to remember that things happen for a reason. It may not be clear to you what it is now, but someday in the future, you will look back at this and understand why they do."

That evening, I stayed up late while my parents were asleep. My tears dried up, and I was emotionally exhausted. In that quiet moment, as I tried to connect with myself and God, I prayed, "Dear God, if this is a challenge you had intended for me, I pray that this is the hardest one you are throwing my way. Please give me strength to overcome this and grant my mother ease as she lives out the rest of her days as you had willed."

As I observed the silence, I heard my voice in my head, "When you hit rock bottom, the only way to go is up."

In the weeks that followed, my mother's health quickly deteriorated. June came around, and she went from losing her basic ability to sit up in bed to suffering seizures as a result of the growing tumour in her brain. I dropped everything I had going on in my life at that time, my brother managed to get some time off work and made it back home, and we made sure that we were together as a family in that hour of need.

We lost my mother on 28 June 2007, a couple of days before her 50th birthday. Her family surrounded her as she took her final breath.

It has been 15 years since she left us. That's 15 years of many personal milestones and significant life events I've gone through without her being around. I've had to learn to deal with the mixed emotions of joy and grief combined each time I have happy news to share with the world because Ibu is no longer just a phone call away.

The process of dealing with the loss of my mother had inevitably been a defining part of my personal growth. Those intense three months of caring for my mother and the couple of years that followed accelerated my journey into adulthood. While my peers were living their best lives as young adults in college, I was figuring out ways to heal the wound and navigate a new world without the person who brought me into it.

What I've come to realise, however, is that losing a loved one is a universal experience. Regardless of whether you lose a parent when you were a child, a teenager, or an adult, many people have to learn to overcome the grief and find a way to move forward in their life after their parent's death.

As I look back on the past 15 years, I attribute my ability to bounce back and find joy again in my life to my strong core support system. And I've come to realise the power of this. Whether it's your sibling, significant other, or group of friends, having a strong and stable support system is significant in helping a grieving person heal and not get lost in the state of bereavement.

For anyone going through a similar experience or dealing with the loss of a loved one, I wish you find your village. And take it from me; the sun will shine in your world again.

About The Author

Rasyida Samsudin Paddy describes herself as a mum, millennial and marketer, "in equal parts".

Coming from a working-class family, Rasyida is a firm believer in the power of education as a great social leveller. She never believed that coming from an ethnic minority or being a woman and a mother should stop her from pursuing a path to success and claiming a social narrative that empowers the communities she represents. She is the youngest of three children and the first college-educated member of her family.

Professionally, Rasyida is an enterprise technology marketing manager with a background in strategic communications and content marketing. She is a proud mother of two girls and considers herself a feminist. Outside of work, Rasyida is passionate about causes that support female representation in the digital economy and spends her time volunteering for organisations whose missions align with this ideal.

You can connect with Rasyida at:

LinkedIn: *https://www.linkedin.com/in/rasyidasam/*

Instagram: *https://www.instagram.com/rasyidapaddy/?hl=en*

Blog: *https://rasyidasam.medium.com/*

STORY SEVEN

Learning and Contribution

What is my Life Mission?

As a little girl, I looked around at the world with my big brown eyes, a smile on my face and felt lightness around me. I remember being a good listener and not wanting to speak because there was so much to watch around me. I remember choosing happiness and joy as a young girl. I say choosing because many things were going on around me that could have pushed me to choose something else.

I grew up in a "typical" suburban middle-income neighbourhood on Long Island, New York. My family, which included myself, my Mom and Dad and my older brother, had a four-bedroom house, a nice yard, two cars, two dogs and a cat. I took all these things for granted as being normal and average.

I went to a public school in my area and loved learning about new things and different places. I had a few good childhood friends but not that many, and I was happy with that. I never felt that I wanted or needed more.

I'm not sure what other people thought about our family because I never asked, but I imagine we seemed like a nice family. But, like many things that look different from the inside than they are on the outside, our family had a lot of "untalked" things that few knew about.

My dear Dad, who I both loved and feared, worked for a plant food company for over 30 years. He loved his work – he spent most evenings in his home office, and he would talk about his work whenever he had a chance. He travelled a lot, and he also drank a lot.

I often wondered why my mom stayed. I sometimes wondered about what it would be like if my mom, brother and I left. It was hard to imagine because my mom wasn't working, and even though my dad drank a lot, she said she still loved him. I didn't quite understand it all then and didn't even try to until much later.

As I got older, my mom would also share that my dad was manic-depressive and on medication that wasn't always working so well. All I knew was that when my dad was drinking, I would lock myself in my bedroom and not come out. My brother, unfortunately, had a more challenging experience during this time.

He was older than me, so I guess he tried to defend my mom. I'm still unclear about what happened during those years, but he still has a lot of anger. I've chosen to forgive, love and look for joy.

I was a top student in high school. I graduated seventh in my class of more than 300 students and went to Swarthmore College, one of the leading small liberal arts schools in the US outside of Philadelphia.

I was on financial aid and also took out student loans, but I felt free. My mom and dad were dedicated to me going to a good school. They always said to me, "Don't worry about how much it will cost. Get into the best school you can, and we will find a way." I am still very grateful for how they dealt with that.

Looking back, I can only now understand how hard that might have been for them. But they still chose abundance over fear. I took that for granted then, but I now realise the true gift my parents gave me.

My college years were great! I was out of the house, and I felt safe. It seemed that many of my friends at college had clearer ideas about what they wanted to do in life. Maybe that's not true, but it felt that way. I didn't feel a real rush either to figure it out. I knew I wasn't motivated by money and felt drawn to helping people. I knew teaching was probably not the right long-term profession for me.

Something else was calling me, like a whisper in my ear, but I couldn't hear it. But it seemed that every time I was at a crossroads and needed to make the next step, something would appear, almost magically. Now, at 53 years old, I can trust that more. I know that the right thing will appear for me when needed, whether it is a person I need to meet, a new client or something I need to learn. It's like magic but better.

When I was in my first semester of senior year at Swarthmore, many friends were applying to Graduate School or preparing their CVs for interviews with companies. I still didn't see a clear picture for myself. I was a Special Studies major in French and International Economics. I had spent my junior year in Grenoble,

France and loved it. It's hard to explain, but it's like France called for me.

And just when I was in my "not knowing", I saw a post through the French Department for an application through the French government to teach English in a French high school. I applied and got it! So there it was, an opportunity given. I didn't need to look for a job. I could go back to my beloved France and explore more.

I had made many friends in Grenoble, so I was excited to return to Europe. I didn't think teaching was the end goal but a fun learning pit-stop along the journey. It ended up being a couple of years pit-stop.

My boyfriend (soon-to-be) husband was a big part of this part of the story. It was a challenging personal time, though. My father had an accident at home, fell off a ladder and almost died. I spent a few months at home and decided to return to France to continue my studies.

It was overwhelming for me to see my dad like this. Not only did he have major physical injuries, his psychiatric medicines got off track, and he was also struggling with depression. I'm not sure how my mom could cope with it all. She was a rock, and I found the stress to be overwhelming.

But I started to feel a yearning for home and the US. I couldn't quite see where or how I would make a living in France, so I told my then fiancé that it was time to return to the USA. He was committed to our relationship and up for the adventure, so he said, "Let's go!"

I'm going to fast-forward this story a bit. We got married, and we went to live in Philadelphia for about five years. My husband worked as a consultant, and through an internship at Eisenhower Fellowships, I landed a job at The International Forum, an executive education program that was part of Wharton at The University of Pennsylvania.

I spent five incredible years travelling around Europe and Asia for my work, meeting CEOs and senior executives from organisations from all parts of the world. It was a truly fantastic experience.

I absolutely loved the job, but it was also one of my most stressful work experiences. I tried so hard to please my boss, which required a level of detail that was not my strength but something I learned I could do well but with a cost to my health. I had unexplained joint problems; my skin was breaking out into hives, and I often felt awful.

My husband had gone back to do his MBA at Wharton, and when he was looking for jobs in his second year, I said to him, "How about going to live in Asia?" I had been spending a lot of my time on projects in China, Thailand and Japan and was fascinated. I had started learning Mandarin and thought, "Now's the time," before having kids. Being a committed adventurer, my husband said, "Sure, let's make it work." Before we knew it, we flew to Singapore to start a new life in Asia.

We only thought it would be for a couple of years. Now, 24 years later, I have two beautiful daughters with my first husband; I started a new career as an executive coach, and then we were separated in 2007 and divorced in 2008. I met my current husband the day my divorce was finalised.

Much of what happened from that time is a bit of a blur. I tend to block out painful things; it's hard to remember all the details before I know it. That was the coping mechanism I learned to stay in my happy bubble as a child. All I know is that through my divorce and the time after, my "invisible" bubble somehow burst.

It was like all the pain I had avoided from childhood, and early adulthood came flooding into my body. I felt sadness like I had never felt before. My first husband told me once that he thought I was heartless.

I think he was right to a certain degree because I didn't allow myself to feel anything until that bubble burst. I walked around with an eternal smile, ensuring everything looked and seemed perfect but not feeling much. I was like an observer of my life but not genuinely experiencing any of it.

As in the past, my coaching path showed up at my doorstep. I was trying to find out what I was meant to be doing in my life, and I met someone who was starting a Leadership Consultancy and Coaching Company. Even though I didn't have any coaching experience, I somehow convinced him to hire me to train someone to run public seminars while he would also start training me as a Coach.

For me, it was like I had found my home. It was an inner sigh of relief to feel that I had finally found a connection to a profession that was and still is authentic to me.

The best part of being a Coach after helping others is that you are also devoted to your own self-development. It's an ongoing journey. So for the past 20-plus years, I have spent endless hours learning more about coaching, people and myself.

At one such training, I met an exceptional coach at a European conference who led a session about expanding your energy, connecting with others and transformational coaching work. This spoke to me. One of his colleagues came to Singapore and started me on the next part of my coaching journey – raising consciousness.

My mission on earth was becoming more apparent. I realised that I am here on this planet to raise humanity's consciousness level. Many others are here now to do the same thing.

I used to hear myself saying this to other coaches, and they probably thought I was a little crazy at the time. But now, I say it without hesitation. I know that the world, humanity, communities, and organisations are going through a shift as we have never seen before.

It is an energetic shift that will change how we live and work. We are moving to a place where we move away from the notion of "separateness" and towards "oneness". This will be filled with courage, authenticity, truth, love, and service to others.

I genuinely believe that we choose to be born on this planet at the soul level. We choose our parents and family for what we are meant to learn to awaken. Then we end up spending years and years, and for some a lifetime, trying to remember why we are here and what we are meant to learn and contribute. I think I am one of the lucky ones. I see the meaning of my life, however, challenging it might seem.

Believe in yourself, your thoughts and your intuition. We are all here for a reason and I encourage all of you to look deep inside yourself and ask what this mission might be. I think we all have 'whispers' of our gifts and many choose life paths that pull us away from these. It is never too late to listen to them and find your journey in this lifetime.

My wish for everyone who reads this is that you look deep inside yourself and ask yourself the question, "What am I meant to be doing here? What is my life mission?".

About The Author

Nancy Hughes, MCC is an Executive Coach with over 25 years of experience in leadership development, including coaching, facilitation and creating executive education programs. Nancy is a global citizen born in the US. She has lived for five years in France, and 24 years in Singapore and now splits her time between Greece, Singapore and the US. Truth and authenticity are at the core of Nancy's belief system and values. She is passionate about supporting others around her to reach their highest potential as leaders and as human beings.

In addition, Nancy is very interested in natural and energy healing, and connecting with like-minded light workers in the world. She is Reiki trained and looks at the world holistically, seeing that we are all connected as energetic beings and impact each other with our thoughts and actions.

Nancy spends most of her free time with family, and close friends and connecting with nature and animals.

You can connect with Nancy at:

Email: *nancy@vincerecoaching.com*

LinkedIn: *https://www.linkedin.com/in/nancy-hughes-912131/*

STORY EIGHT

Learning the Art of Saying "No"

The story of a girl with zero confidence, to someone who helps people to gain their confidence back.

Did you know that no one is born confident?

Self-confidence is something that can be learned as one goes through life's experiences and faces challenges.

When you push those boundaries and go that extra mile, it helps you feel good about yourself and starts you on that first step to feeling self-confident. It sounds simple but is hard to put into practice and accomplish. However, with the proper guidance and work, it can be achieved.

Having worked as a lawyer for five years and then an executive/life coach and speaker for seven years with over 500 hours of coaching 150+ clients across Asia-Pacific, one assumes that being confident would come naturally to me. But, that is not the case. I had to learn and develop the skill of self-confidence through my journey of experiences.

My story is that of a girl who was extremely low on self-confidence for most of her life and how through life's experiences, she learnt to stand up for herself and gain confidence. The story has its fair share of highs and lows, ups and downs and even though I have miles to go, I'm grateful for the lessons learned and how it's all panned out so far.

Growing up, I was very low on self-confidence, definitely a follower and not a leader. I did not believe I needed to follow my heart or my dreams and probably lacked the courage to do so anyway. I lived a regular life while trying to excel at work and make my family happy. While not miserable, at least I do not think I was, I was indeed not living up to my potential. After completing my bachelor's degree in commerce, I pursued law and qualified as a lawyer. After that, I married at 24 in the traditional Indian "arranged marriage" setup.

It was not the kind of union I had expected, as my husband and I were polar opposites. We disagreed on almost every aspect of our lives. I was miserable and felt stuck in a marriage without respect and with plenty of abuse. The strain and stress were affecting me mentally and physically. I had begun coughing incessantly, waking up at night choking, unable to lie down or eat most foods and lost about seven to eight kilos. This condition would not abate even after months of medications and added to my misery in an already troubled relationship.

However, this sickness turned out to be the turning point for me. Doctors diagnosed that I had developed chronic acid reflux primarily due to stress. Then, I decided to take charge of my life and turn it around. My life was too important, and I could not waste it away like this in sickness and misery.

Ending my marriage seemed like a mammoth task. There appeared to be too much at stake, apart from the fact that I was fearful of the outcome and had no visibility of my future. The thought of all the effort required to restart and rebuild my life seemed arduous. Nevertheless, one thing was crystal clear – my desire to live a happy, fulfilled life.

Finally, after years of suffering and being unable to stand up for myself, I said "NO" and decided to free myself from the shackles of my so-called "destiny". It felt like I had achieved something great by saying "No" to an unhappy life, saying "No" to disrespect and saying "No" to abuse.

That is where the problem lies. Saying "No" with confidence should have been a natural way forward; however, most individuals tend to put another's objectives before theirs, and that's what I had done as well. With this mindset, self-confidence is difficult, and it takes tremendous courage even when one is suffering.

It was the best decision of my life! It was very uncharacteristic and a massive step for me. I had changed forever and realised I had a second chance at life, and I was determined to make the most of it. I owed it to myself! Many people applauded me then and continue to do so even after all these years.

However, I felt empty inside. It was extremely challenging since I was also battling depression, but I believed that I and my life were too precious a gift to waste away in misery. I had to force myself to focus on all the abundance and be grateful for it, which seemed impossible then, but I needed to do all it took to get back on my feet.

I was a voracious reader who researched my condition, found various self-help techniques, and worked with healers and therapists. I was recommended the simple practice of writing affirmations by one of my therapists.

Affirmations are powerful, positive statements written in the present tense that allow you to be in control of your thoughts consciously.

Research has shown that around 80% of the 50,000 subconscious thoughts you have daily are negative. That is a lot of negativity! Therefore, when you consciously think positive thoughts, it is easier to control the negative ones that constantly threaten to take over. To affirm is to say something positive. I would always be writing or speaking to myself – I am free, I am happy, I am alive. It almost felt like I was possessed saying all these positive things while I felt miserable and far from positive. But the magic happened!

I started feeling much better and happier. It was odd. My environment had not changed, but I was feeling more in control. It took time but eventually, I garnered the courage and finally ended the union that was choking me. My acid reflux took years to diminish, but it finally did. I had to overcome various fears and hurdles to finally learn to be self-confident.

My biggest strength and weapon I realised was the belief in myself (backed by the love of my family and other loved ones), the belief that I am worth it and important.

Another practice I followed was the most critical factor in shifting my mindset from a fixed fear mindset to one of freedom, with a growth mindset.

I would like to call it the "Inside Out Mantra", which is based on the paradigm that our environment is a reflection of us. Further, our mind is our best helper and supporter, allowing us to lead the life of our dreams. So if you want to change your environment, you need to change something within you and change your focus. We have no control over anything other than ourselves, which most individuals forget. Hence, to trigger the inside-out mantra, you need to take charge and responsibility instead of blaming external factors.

So when I wanted to leave a loveless marriage, instead of blaming everyone involved, it happened only when I took charge and decided that I had to improve my life on my own.

What I also realised was that our most potent allies are:

- the written words and
- our imagination.

Writing or journaling is the most powerful tool at our disposal. It's an outlet we all need to help rid us of the crap accumulated in our minds, not allowing the good stuff to come into our lives. When we write, we also engage all our senses – visual, kinaesthetic and auditory, triggering our unconscious mind to start doing the work for us. That is step one – painting a clear picture by way of words of what we want to manifest in our lives.

Step two is visualising the life we ultimately want to achieve and live. Our imagination and thoughts have the power to create our reality. Visualising our dream life in elaborate detail helps our unconscious mind by giving exact instructions of what it needs to do for us. It cannot differentiate between reality or something that is imagined.

The unconscious mind understands abstract and not logic. Logic is for the conscious mind. Hence repeating the act of visualising or imagining your dream or goal is good enough instruction for the unconscious mind to start doing the work. Be sure to focus on every specific detail of your goal so that the unconscious mind has clear instructions on what to do. Visualise that you have already achieved what you are dreaming of, and it will come into your life sooner.

This is an old trick used by athletes who visualise themselves at the finish line as winners and running the entire race in their mind before they actually do it. The process assists the mind in delivering what the athlete wants.

If you cannot visualise your dream or goal, there is a low chance of you achieving it, so see yourself as a winner in every aspect of your life, and you will succeed!

The goal was to be happy again. And it's ok not to experience magic automatically, so I feverishly worked on triggering my visual, auditory and kinaesthetic senses to help me get the courage to achieve this goal. Sometimes I did not believe it would work, but I was so desperate to be happy again that I worked hard on my inside to change my outside environment, and it finally happened!

I had used my mind, support from professionals and a bit of science to help me stand up for myself confidently and begin to turn my life around. I am now married with two beautiful children, living the life of my dreams on my terms!

Take back the remote control of your life and be the only one in charge of it! Life is too short to waste even a single day being anything but happy!

It has been a fantastic journey for me – transforming from a girl with zero confidence to someone who helps people regain their confidence! It has been exhausting and exhilarating, to say the least, but I am grateful for every experience because it has made me the person I always dreamed of becoming.

Hence, I encourage you to lead your best life with happiness and confidence. I believe that we all have a mission in our lives that guides the journey we take. Some of us are self-aware, others less so. My mission is to help you become more self-aware, learn to be confident and happy and define what "having it all" means for you instead of what the world has told you it should be.

If you ever read about Ziauddin Yousafzai – Nobel Prize-winning Malala Yousafzai's father, he was asked umpteen times about what he did to make her what she is today. His answer simply was, "It's not what I did, but what I did not do, and that was not to clip her wings and allow her to fly", which I believe gave her the confidence to stand up for herself.

If you want to start on the journey of gaining self-confidence, give yourself permission and allow yourself to fly!

About The Author

Ruchi Parekh is a PCC certified Executive/Life Coach, NLP Practitioner, Keynote Speaker, Accredited Belbin Facilitator and Lawyer based in Singapore.

She helps high-potential professionals build emotional resilience and a positive mindset to get to the next level in their lives personally and professionally.

Her main objective is to help clients move forward and find fulfilment and success in all the roles they play. Guiding individuals through a transition is part of this process, making them feel empowered and accomplished. Her coaching style is results-oriented, ensuring clients experience a paradigm shift that allows them to achieve results in their professional and personal lives. Ruchi has worked with leaders in various industries, including but not limited to financial services, legal, medical, media, technology and human resources.

Ruchi is a winner of the Emerging Executive Coach of the year 2022 Award. She was also featured in the *Asian Money Guide* amongst the 50 power women of Asia.

You can connect with Ruchi at:

Email: *hello@ruchiparekh.com*

Website: *www.ruchiparekh.com*

Linkedin: *www.linkedin.com/in/ruchmadan81*

STORY NINE

Life's Journey to an Unexpected Destination

Lessons are learned along a journey, so let us fully embrace the fulfilment of the destination when we eventually arrive.

When I was a young girl, I never wanted to get married or have children, convinced this held women back from achieving their life ambitions. My goals were to have an international career, climb the proverbial corporate ladder, travel to experience different cultures, and make a difference as a champion of women's empowerment.

Today, thirty years on, I find myself a wife, mother, and global corporate leader. Did life's journey just take me here? Did I wake up one morning and say, "What happened?!" As someone who plans everything, the answer is a resounding "No". Every decision I made, and every step I've taken has been thoughtful and intentional, with some pivots along the way.

As I look back at my life journey, there were several key moments and decision points, which have hugely influenced who and where I am today.

Moment #1: Choose "the one" who respects and supports your personal goals

Born in Singapore, I was raised by a strong mother with deep Asian values about family and work ethic. She also inculcated in me a strong sense of independence and self-sufficiency.

I met my husband (then boyfriend) at 19 while at university in Australia. I was extremely driven, studying hard and working part-time to support myself, with progressive opinions about relationships. On our third date, I decided to make my life goals clear to him -- career first, wife and mother never. Oh, for good measure, I also threw in not cooking, cleaning, or doing any expected 'womanly' household duties. Instead of running out the door as I fully expected, he said, "Ok", and that was the start of a relationship that has lasted 30 years, including 23 years of marriage.

As our relationship progressed, I came around to the idea that marriage would not (as I initially thought) stand in the way of achieving my life goals. I encountered many challenges in those early career years, and I believe it was his respect for my independence and personal ambition that played a key role in my not being deterred from my desired path. His career stability and maturity (being six years older) gave me a safe space from which to make risky (albeit calculated) career decisions.

Moment #2: Set early career goals and don't hold yourself back from going for it

Starting my career in a market research agency at age 25, I set myself the goal of making it to Director level by age 30. I had spent three years completing a PhD in Marketing and was a few years behind my peers. Hence, I worked tirelessly to make up for this perceived "lost time" (don't ask me why I was in such a rush), resulting in an accelerated career path to manager.

The first big career opportunity came my way at the end of 2002 when I was offered a Global Director position at my company's UK headquarters. At some point during the all-important interview with the boss of my boss' boss, he asked about my career ambition, to which I shared "to become a Director by age 30". My response to his next question of how much time I had, was "four days", which elicited an amused reaction about "cutting it rather close". Three days later, he offered me the job, a day before my 30th birthday, so I could achieve my goal. Twenty years later, I still recall the poignancy of that moment, particularly as the corporate environment was not very people-oriented at that time, as opposed to today.

That interview was only the first hurdle I encountered, as others soon surfaced to deter me from pursuing the opportunity. I was newly married, would my husband find a job in London? My father suddenly passed away, should I leave my mother alone in Singapore?

This was my first life experience with the many hurdles or questions in your head, that women encounter every time we wish to pursue our own dreams and aspirations. We are often our worst critics and enemies. Thankfully, I had the inner strength and external support of close family and friends, to not be shaken or deterred! I moved to London with my husband in tow (who found a job in London, incidentally), to pursue my career dream.

Moment #3: Baby will rock your world, but hang in there

The work experience in the UK was akin to being thrown into the deep end to sink or swim, and I absolutely thrived and embraced it! Up to this moment, my life journey was defined by lots of hard work, with things going relatively smoothly to plan.

Then in 2004, came a major event that shook my world in the shape of a gorgeous and intelligent baby girl, who essentially imploded my up-till-then, perfectly planned life. I had (of course) set myself the goal of 100% breastfeeding for six months, although I returned to work after four months to a demanding job with significant travel. I spent my first day at work post-maternity running around the building, locating the nursing room to express, the fridge to store milk, and hot water to sterilise the equipment, all in between work meetings. When the day ended, I went home, picked up my baby and cried.

I was definitely shaken but refused to be deterred. That fateful day would be a sign of what was to come for the next ten years. Balancing a demanding career with raising children, and working in corporate environments that were not always family-friendly, while also maintaining a happy marriage… was really hard work! My career that I had worked so hard for was on a steep trajectory, yet I loved these children, who needed my time and attention. Thinking back, I have no regrets. While extremely challenging and exhausting, becoming a mother has fulfilled me in ways I could not have imagined, turning me into the more holistic and caring individual I am today.

Juggling several balls in the air daily, I was constantly shaken and stirred. However, I constantly reminded myself not to forget the aspirations I had before I became a mother. Although on some days, surviving on two hours of sleep was really, just… too… hard.

Moment #4: There's no need to be a hero, it takes a Village to raise a child

Enter…. my "Village", of which the Chief is my mother. There is a good reason for the saying, "It takes a village to raise a child". My village of support has been instrumental in allowing me to manage work and family these 18+ years.

My mother was my first female role model, a strong woman who fought through childhood poverty to build a successful business in China while raising a family. Even though I am grateful to my father for my academic genes, my business acumen and EQ definitely come from my mother. When I became a parent myself, my mother retired to help raise my two daughters, managing the household and home help. Her support enabled my husband and me to spend quality time with our girls and each other, enjoying a blissful family life as the children grew up.

In 2006, I made the hard but right decision to return to Singapore where I had my village of support, a decision that effectively decelerated my steep career trajectory. Undeterred, I used the next ten years to develop myself in other leadership skills which have proven critical in my position today, such as managing through ambiguity, agility, people management and more.

Along a woman's journey to "have it all", a career, happy marriage, and children, it is mind-blowing how many hurdles still exist today, in both society and the corporate world. I have found myself overcoming countless hurdles, while actively tuning out well-meaning but unhelpful comments. Hurdles that would not exist if I were a man, comments that amplified the negative thoughts in my head to not pursue my own ambition, as it was not putting the family first.

Moment #5: A deliberate career pause or pivot need not derail your ambition forever

The next big career opportunity that came my way, took immense planning and resilience to overcome all obstacles to move the family to Paris. The children were now older, and I had shared with my husband my readiness for an overseas career move.

As much as I portray the image of being extremely focused on my career, I genuinely endeavour to do it always with my family in mind. When presented with this massive career opportunity, I still deliberated because of the potential impact on my husband's career and children's education. "Aren't there terrorists everywhere in Paris", "what about your husband's job", and "your children will get derailed overseas", were some of the well-meaning comments I received.

Thankfully, I had my closest female friends who kept me moving forward. Together we made a list of all potential hurdles to find solutions to, so I was not deterred from pursuing my first C-level role. I am ever grateful to this extended-Village friend group, who serves as my sounding board, ever constructive and never judgemental.

Moment #6: Unbeknownst to me, the biggest challenge was around the corner

The support of this extended-Village became critical when I faced my greatest challenge – working and solo parenting through a pandemic, without domestic support, in a new country.

Moving to my current job in the UK at the end of 2019 was meant to be a huge win-win opportunity for our family. It was a chance for me to do my "dream" job at the company I walked away from 15 years ago for personal and family reasons. My husband would finally end his long-distance commute from Singapore as he could practise medicine in the UK, which he was not able to do in Paris due to EU regulations. Attending a top UK high school would boost the chances of my older daughter achieving her Oxford childhood dream. My younger daughter would continue in an international education environment better suited to her than the more stringent (albeit extremely good) Singaporean system.

Then COVID-19 threw a giant spanner in my best-laid plans. It was fine at first, as I made the snap decision in March 2020 with the support of my manager, to yank both girls out of school, and fly home overnight to reunite as a family. Hence, we were able to see through the worst of the first lockdown in the safety net that was Singapore.

Riding out the next 18 months in London proved to be much harder, as I was separated from the domestic support of my mother and husband for an extended time. Solo parenting two teenage girls (one who was going through Sixth Form/University preparation), through a long four-month lockdown in London, at a time when hospitals were overloaded, and I was the only adult responsible for their well-being... I wasn't just shaken... I was scared! But, I had to maintain a brave, strong front.

Post-lockdown and with vaccinations, things brightened. Until another massive quake shook my world, and I finally hit a wall. I ran out of energy, mental, emotional and physical. I could not breathe, I could not go on. Yet somehow, I had to find the strength from somewhere deep within me. I refused to be deterred.

Thinking back, I feel truly blessed by the support I received at this toughest of moments. Firstly, it was a genuine career first for me to call my manager to say "I'm going through a hard time and need time to myself." His immediate support and reminder to me about "the extraordinary professional" I am, gave me the reassurance to take more time off over the summer to rest, reflect, spend time reunited as a family, and recover my energy. Secondly, my friends provided positive shots of energy to recharge my batteries, virtually long-distance or in person. I returned much more myself post-summer, ready to take on the world again.

I had been extremely shaken. Stirred....like in a whirlpool! But, Deterred? Never!!!

The Journey Continues

My story started with how I wanted to be a global corporate leader, not a wife or mother.

Yet somehow, through the highs and lows of my life journey, I have to my genuine surprise, discovered myself to be a better mother and wife than I thought myself possible to ever be. At the same time, I am where I aspired to be in my career, a global corporate leader and champion of women's empowerment.

People often say to me, "Elaine, you make it all look so easy". To be clear: it was never easy, even if it looked that way.

Perhaps, like the title of this book, being Shaken and Stirred is the path to finding the best version of yourself. I somehow have, and my wish is that each one of you, will find the best version of yourself, and go live your best life ever.

About The Author

Elaine Rodrigo is doing her 'dream job' at Reckitt, as Chief Insights & Analytics Officer. She leads both the consumer insights and data analytics teams across the entire organisation.

She has more than 20 years of experience transforming insights functions in the FMCG industry across multinational corporations including Reckitt, Danone and Mondelez/Kraft Foods, and global research agencies. Living and working in Singapore, Australia, UK and France, has equipped her with the agility to pivot and transform organisations, even in an ever-changing and ambiguous corporate environment.

In addition to her day job, Elaine sits on the Board of a Swedish tech start-up and is a mother to two beautiful, free-thinking daughters. Never forgetting her academic roots, Elaine has a PhD in Marketing from Monash University in Australia, where she is also a Fellow, and works closely with Oxford University as part of their Future of Marketing Initiative (FOMI).

You can connect with Elaine at:

Email: *elainerodrigo@yahoo.com*

LinkedIn: *https://www.linkedin.com/in/elaine-rodrigo-3b25b84/*

STORY TEN

Line in the Sand

At forty, my priority became me and continues to be me, myself, and I.

I've always wanted to narrate a fraction of my story. Maybe for myself as my memory keeps drifting away or perhaps just to share what I think is interesting and inspiring.

One soul in this world is ready to start. To start what? Maybe to create what you dreamed of? Maybe to start differently from yesterday and harvest a different result today. I don't know.

I am writing now to inspire ordinary humans like me – not famous, but hesitant, confused sometimes, with kids, single mothers, hard workers, holding two jobs or more, wondering how to pay the bills and how to help their kids to keep going with the online study thing that they don't understand themselves.

This chapter is for those of us who think that they aren't talented enough to affect a single soul out of the eight billion people on Earth. This chapter is dedicated to me, my daughters, and all the girls and women out there who need a light at the end of their tunnels.

Why women? Well, because I am a woman and I know about our struggles, challenges and self doubts. I know what makes us tick and what doesn't. I know what makes us happy and what makes us sad. I know how we see ourselves when we look in the mirror. I see the pain behind those eyes even when the mouth is smiling. I see you because I am you. And this very well may be your story too.

Forty was the age I woke up to myself and decided to help myself. It was the discovery of "The New Me". It was the "click" in my head of a door opening, and I am glad I walked through.

My life can be split into two significant chapters – before 40 and after 40.

You may think I was involved in a major accident for my world to be so shaken and to cause the dramatic changes that I deserved. But no, that was not the case. My decision to lose weight was made in a surreal moment while walking my eldest daughter to school.

I know! Not as many would expect, but that's the truth. It was the breaking point of my life. The moment I finally decided to invest in myself, in my body and in sport (the least of my interests at that time).

I was breathing heavily, as always, but it was different and more difficult that morning. It was at that moment I made a life-changing decision. Sure, I had thought about losing weight many times before but somehow the feeling was never as strong as it was that day.

Having been overweight for most of my life, it somehow defined who I was. I was not happy with who I was but never cared enough to do something about it. But now I was finally convinced to spend some money on myself.

The money I worked long hours for and generously spent on others rather than fixing myself. I made room in the budget for my sport alongside the queue of other bills – utilities, school, rent, kids' requirements, car loans, etc.

I took this colossal step towards self-investment without feeling that I was a "selfish mother" or a "lavish partner" (at that time), or even a "stingy friend". I was so generous to others but not to myself. My priority became me and continues to be me, myself, and I, with zero motherly guilt.

I reduced my weight from 110 kg to 45 kg! I went from treating food as a "lover" to treating food as an "enemy". I went from extreme obesity and a Body Mass Index (BMI) of 49.9 to extremely skinny with a BMI below 20.

Both sides are scary and confusing – to be fat or to be skinny. Both didn't feel right. It took me a few years to finally adjust and align the picture of my body inside my head with what I see in the mirror. I finally reached what I sought – the physical balance in my life – without any extremes.

Food isn't my lover anymore nor my worst enemy. Food is just fuel and an energy source for my body to function. There is no emotion linked to food.

To maintain the new me that I reached was, and still is, difficult.

We don't live in isolation; hence we affect and get affected. I had to make significant changes to my lifestyle, starting with changing my environment, the friends I hung out with, the food choices I made, the timing and hours of my sleep and the way I thought of my body and the activities I was doing. It became a long whole-of-life checklist.

What surprised me and disappointed me was the non-acceptance of my new lifestyle by many of my relatives and so-called friends. When I bump into some of these people, they tell me they prefer the old fat Omaimaa. Crazy ha! I stick to my beliefs and do what I want and have always wanted to do.

That's a fraction of my life but a major one. That's simply the "Me Now" and the "Me Then" – Being and Balancing. My weight loss journey was 50 percent of my getting my life back. You might now be wondering what the other 50 percent might be.

Turning forty was the light at the end of the tunnel for me. It was the age when something clicked inside me, unlocking my human dimensions on the journey towards self-discovery.

"To start, to begin is the start of the choice of changing. We all need to start because it is a need and a necessity, not a luxury. It is the resilience to renewal to relevance with the continuous changes we face in our cycles of life."
– Sadhguru

To explain, I refer to and define the difficulties of self-changing as layers. There were layers of heavy loads literally above me and my head. That's how I see it.

After I achieved complete control of my "body weight" layer, things became easier for me to handle. The weight loss process equipped me with excellent focusing skills and lifted my inner self to a higher level of confidence than I had ever witnessed or felt.

The space left by things and people no longer in my life was immense and running and sports weren't enough to fill it. I needed more.

I was like a re-born child witnessing new things for the first time in life, and yes, that is at more than 40 years old!

What can a decade (now I am 50) do to recover a wasted 40 years of life? I was living life jumping and not simply walking or running. I was eager to discover and try everything I missed in my childhood, teenage years and certainly part of my adulthood.

Everything was a "WOW" to me, just like a child, and at all levels of life. I was trying new clothing styles, eating new food, dealing with new nationalities, playing new games, discussing new subjects, trying new colours and hairstyles, having new adventures, connecting with nature, to mountains and deserts, and learning to swim (since I had a phobia about swimming), touching a dog (again since I have a zoo phobia), putting myself into different discomfort zones almost every weekend. It never stopped.

Life became more colourful with different flavours and spices. People often ask me on social media where I get all this energy. This includes my few new friends and running mates, and I tell them that because I am exploring new things in life, and what is left of my life may be less than what has already been, I have no more time to waste.

Finding the right Life Coach was the next step. Surprisingly things fall into place quickly when we set a genuine intention. Asking for help is another level of consciousness with which I have always had a problem. It always felt to me that seeking assistance was putting a burden on others.

With the help of my Life Coach I was beginning to see things differently. Investing in my inner self was another "layer of change" I adopted. It also filled the space losing the old me had left. Life was looking great!

Then, last night I was reborn. It seemed I was supposed to finish this new part of my life here, but ironically, I was fighting for my breath, fighting for my life.

I was immediately admitted to the Emergency Room and was diagnosed with an electrolyte imbalance which led to irregular high heartbeats and anxiety. I stayed there the whole night fighting for my life. And when I woke up the next morning, it literally was a wake-up call.

Since being menopausal for the last two years, my body was already challenged. On top of that, my poor nutrition and being too busy lately to eat a single full meal. I depended on caffeine and was not hydrating enough. I had abused my body to the limit and finally it gave in.

It was a lesson. An expensive one, but I am genuinely grateful for the second chance I have been given. It is a colossal wake-up call, and I shall take it seriously. The first step was quitting mobile phones and social media to spend more time with my two daughters.

I am at home now, watching TV, writing the rest of this chapter, and taking it easy. Though I am OK now, I must regularly visit the hospital for monitoring and check-ups. I spend my day resting at home, cooking, reading a book and welcoming dear friends. Life is so easy this way and much more relaxing.

You think that you have taught your children how to behave or react when such an unexpected event occurs, but trust me, we are never ready for any unexpected actions that mess with our life's routine.

The idea of being a strong single mother is not on my mind anymore and shouldn't have been in my kid's minds. We always need help and need trustworthy people around us.

The Omaimaa who started writing this chapter is different from the Omaimaa writing it now. My whole perspective on life has changed. My priorities, my lifestyle and even my daily habits have changed. It is strange, scary and unbelievable how your life can turn upside down in a day. No, let me rephrase that – in a blink of an eye. A 180-degree change can occur in your life without plans and rehearsal.

It can be a sudden movement, like an earthquake, fast and deeply shaken, a fast and sudden shake, an intense one.

Please take my story as a lesson. Do not take your life and your relationships for granted. Stay healthy and hug your loved ones every day.

About The Author

Omaimaa Mohammad was a banker for 25 years until the start of the COVID-19 pandemic. It was then she decided to share her life experiences, passion for sport and the outdoors along with her desire to help other women follow her path to complete fullness.

Her business Ikigai Lifestyle Coaching (ILC) was born in UAE in July 2020. It focuses exclusively on women's health enabling women to find purpose in their lives and day-to-day living.

ILC's primary role is to guide, mentor, and assist women to find better versions of themselves through hiking and outdoor activities and lifestyle changes.

You can connect with Omaimaa at:

LinkedIn: *http://linkedin.com/in/omaimaa-mo-5564bb5*

Twitter: *http://Twitter.com/OmaimaaMohammad*

Instagram: *https://www.instagram.com/omaimaamohammad/*

STORY ELEVEN

Loss and Awakening

If you are in a position to help someone else, you are blessed.

When I was approached to share my story, I was not sure if I should. After all, I am not a writer. I am a financial planner. This made me realise that I am a lot of other things – a mother, daughter, sister, sister-in-law, wife, friend, ex-girlfriend, boss, and colleague. But wait, these are all roles I play in this life, not who I am.

Then who am I?

Am I the person that lives in this body who doesn't ever let me give up, or am I that feeling that does not allow me to waiver from my focus, no matter what comes my way – always bouncing back to happiness no matter what?

I remember my mother being that person who would always stay happy no matter what life threw at her. She used to say, "Whatever went wrong is already in the past, and you cannot change it, so why cry over it? Move on and save what you still have while you have it. Be in gratitude that whatever bad happened stopped at that. It could have been a lot worse. That Supreme Being (God/The Universe) is watching for you. He will always do what is in your best interest."

Or sometimes I wonder if I am that person who can dump anything for the call of duty. Duty is supreme, and nothing must deter me from that path. More spiritually speaking, duty is Dharma. It can be professional or personal. Whatever its nature, the core message always remains the same – others over self. I remember my father was that kind of a person.

I am probably a mix of the two. Whoever I am, I know the one thing that I am not.

I am NOT deterred, which is probably why I agreed to contribute to this book.

My story is like a Bollywood saga. There is more drama in my life than in many movies in the Indian film industry. I am confident that if a famous director were to get a hold of my life story, they could draw out more masala (a highly varied mix of elements) for their movies. I agreed to write my story only so I could inspire others. People who feel the balance in their lives have been upset, given the lemons that life has constantly thrown at them. Guys, just don't give up.

My father was in the Government Services, and we were amongst the privileged class. He was a highly respected officer with a career full of adventurous stories, just like in the movies. Our mother was a school teacher and did a great job keeping my brother and me grounded. She even taught in the same school we studied in.

You can understand that it is as grounded as you can get. No gossip would ever come our way. We always had to be the good kids – at home and in school.

I started my professional journey in the financial services industry around two decades ago. This was when I was preparing for the civil services exams.

I saw first-hand the impact adequate life insurance cover had on the lives of a family that my family was very close to. The breadwinner died suddenly in a freak accident, leaving behind two children aged two and six months, a wife who had given up work after the children were born and his parents who were dependent on his income.

But to our surprise, there was no change in the lifestyle of this family, except that the wife had to take up working again. Later we learned that the reason for the family's comfortable lifestyle despite the huge loss was because of meticulous life insurance planning. This inspired me to change my path, joining the insurance sector. It was difficult for me to convince my family owing to the multiple prejudices against this profession, but I managed.

This is the only decision I have ever made for myself, and I have no clue what drove me to do this. My family always made all my life decisions. This included the subjects I would take in school, the clothes I would wear, the friends I had, and the man I would marry. But on this one decision, I stood my ground. Luckily, one thing led to another, and I made a decent career in the Life Insurance industry.

2021 was an excessively eventful year for me. Professionally, I had an incredible start to the financial year. I was given a new team to work with. Unfortunately, however, my parents were not doing too well medically. As luck would have it, my father, a kidney transplant patient, started having trouble and passed away on 22 July 2021.

Just four days before this, on 18 July 2021, I was delivering a talk on women's empowerment and financial literacy. A conversation with a participant during this talk changed something inside me.

I suddenly wanted to change how things were for me. I wanted to share this with my father as he was the one I trusted. He was my pillar of strength and anchor in this scary and mysterious world.

Anything that I was not sure of, I could run it past him once, and everything would start to make so much more sense. Unfortunately, this thing that had changed inside me was so big that I wanted to be sure before sharing it with him. Since he was not doing too well, I thought I'll share once he returns from the hospital.

Unfortunately, he passed away, and I did not get a chance to speak with him. But my resolve became stronger throughout the 13 days of mourning and all the religious chants being played at home, and I parted ways with my husband.

This shook one part of my world. On the other hand, my mother was not doing well either, and I saw her health deteriorating. After my father died, it was almost like she had lost her will to live. And within 90 days of his death, on 21 October, she decided to leave us to rest in his arms forever.

This devastated both my brother and me.

In life, I believe you have people in circles around you. The circle closest to you are the people you live with – your family members, including your kids, spouse, parents, siblings and sometimes close friends. The next circle are your other close relatives, friends, etc. I am sure you understand what I am trying to say.

In 90 days, I had lost 90 per cent of my first circle. My parents were gone, and I had left my husband and the house I had lived in for the last 21 years. I just did not know how to cope. I would cry day and night.

My daughter had never seen me in such chaos. One day, my daughter, after seeing me in shambles, said to me, "Mom, I need you to pull yourself out of this mode. We need you here." These words helped me snap out of my misery.

She showed me a clip from the Hindi movie *Queen*. In it, the lead actress Kangana is sozzled and is sitting and crying in front of strangers.

"Mera life itna kharaab ho gaya……mera life itna kharaab ho gaya…." (*My life is ruined ……. My life is ruined*)

I was in fits of laughter. I understood how life was waiting to happen for me while I was crying over what was in the past. I was doing precisely the reverse of what my parents had always taught me.

I also realised through this whole never-ending loop of my thinking that God was hard on me that I was missing how my daughter was going through a miserable time herself. She was dealing with all I was dealing with as she had also lost her maternal grandparents. She suddenly had two houses, her class 10 board exams were coming up, and she was dealing with anxiety affecting her mental health.

My baby wanted a mother, and she played at being my mother. But that day, the drama ended. I decided to put a stop to the self-pitying, victim mode. My daughter got her mother back, and my practice got its professional back.

I soon realised that:

- **I was now living my life by myself, and this is how it will be from now on**. This was my choice. I had never had that before. I used to wake up to someone telling me what to do. I had never lived alone. I had never slept alone in a house. I had never done all of this by myself. I had always lived with my parents and then after I got married, with my husband and in-laws.
- **I had to take care of my daughter all by myself.** (Yes, her dad was chipping in his part, but I had to be the Mother that I always had been, but she needed more of me at this time. She required her strong mother. My baby had gone through a lot just like me.)
- **I had to excel at my practice. It was not a choice anymore.** I had to scale up this practice (at a faster pace than ever before) if I wanted to survive alone.

> I had been working for almost two decades but never had I ever been able to scale it to the levels that I now desired.

As they say, you win some, and you lose some. I had lost enough. I knew losing more was not an option. And that is when the tables started to turn for me. I could suddenly see friends stretching out their hands to help me that I did not see before. I knew I was not alone anymore.

I was healing. And my relationship with my daughter grew into being that of best friends.

My practice was the more difficult part, but then I realised if the best sports people can have coaches, then why can't I? Fortunately, I found myself a coach in no time. I feel proud that my practice is now on track and growing at a pace that pleases me.

Today, I am amongst the few top earners and contributors to the business of a leading life insurance company in India. In addition, I have been able to link a social cause to my practice, giving me that extra push to work. We adopt villages in the interiors of states like Jharkhand, Chhattisgarh, and Bihar Madhya Pradesh and try to solve the villagers' daily problems.

It is my way of contributing, big or small. My father used to say that if you are in a position to help someone, you are blessed and not doing anyone favours. The superior powers have assigned you that task, and it is your duty to assist.

I am not saying I don't have those down times anymore – I still do.

I feel lonely, sad and jealous of others, and then I go back to counting my blessings and realise that I may have been shaken by the turn of events in my life this last year. But I could not be deterred from living a life of fulfilment, both professionally and personally.

I know I am walking the path my parents would have liked me to walk, and it will be in peace when I die.

Life will shake you, stir you, and rough you around in many ways, but at the same time, it will always leave that one rope, that one silver lining for you, so that you don't get deterred.

For me, it is my daughter.

About The Author

Pallavi Chaturvedi is a life insurance professional with a leading insurer in India and also the Founding Director of BLUEESTONE Wealth Matters Pvt Ltd, a leading personal wealth management company based in New Delhi, India.

She has more than 18 years of experience in the financial services industry and is a Certified Financial Planner (CFP). She began working as a life insurance specialist and then graduated to being a well-known and qualified holistic financial coach. She has worked with more than 17,000 families on future financial security in her journey this far.

Pallavi's specific vision with BLUEESTONE is to extend financial planning services to every household in India by making it affordable and easily accessible to the average Indian citizen.

In fulfilling this mission, the company has worked with varied corporations, NGOs, Public Sector organisations, and paramilitary forces on employee welfare programs targeted toward financial planning.

A lesser-known fact about Pallavi is that she was a national-level swimmer and has a keen interest in all forms of art – painting, sketching, clay modelling, and photography to name but a few.

You can connect with Pallavi at:

Website: *https://pallavichaturvedi.com/*

LinkedIn: *https://www.linkedin.com/in/pallavi-chaturvedi/*

Facebook: *https://www.facebook.com/pallavi.chaturvedi.96*

STORY TWELVE

My Choice

I dreamt it, I wished it, I did it…

Growing Up

I grew up in the city of Mysore in the south of India. I'm the rebellious fourth child in a family of eight children with five brothers and two sisters. My father was a well-respected and well-known craftsman and owned a large handicrafts business with many international customers.

I was a female child born into an orthodox Tamilian family. Family bonding and religious rituals were the priority and the core of all our activities. Our family was like many other Indian households where all the women were homemakers, and the men were the breadwinners. This philosophy was ingrained in us from a young age.

My brothers grew up always behaving like extremely protective bodyguards to their sisters. While I valued their love and protection at times, I also envied their freedom to do anything they wanted.

As the girls of the family, we were "supposed" to not be opinionated or make important decisions of our own, and it was just expected that we would follow the rules at home. Despite these rules and expectations, I never stopped being who I was. I remember looking at my brother as early as five years old, thinking, "If he can do it, why can't I?"

I never restrained myself from getting into fights with my brothers, whether racing them on a bicycle or getting into trouble. I always followed my heart. I always felt that if I could dream it, I could do it. Looking back now, I realise that the strong-mindedness of my brothers had a large part to play in how I viewed myself as passionate, confident, ambitious, courageous and a go-getter.

I still remember my mom reminding us to behave like girls and learn to cook and clean. While I loved cooking, it always baffled me why there were separate rules for boys and girls. Why did the boys always get to do all the fun things like going out, and why did we girls have to stay home?

I dared to question my parents and elders, and all I got for my courage was not exactly how I liked it and that made me even more rebellious and persistent in trying to do what I wanted. It was a given that the accepted life path for girls was to find a husband, and that was the only goal. My relatives constantly reminded me that learning how to cook and run a home was far more valuable than getting good grades. For us reading this now, it must sound so old-fashioned.

I am, however, very grateful to my father, who was a dynamic man. He gave us the best education and always, deep down, drove us to be go-getters and, in this process, imparted me with a solid work ethic and determination. My father was, in many ways, forward-thinking and always believed strongly that education was essential, but all you needed was confidence and ambition.

He sent all eight of us to an international boarding school in Ooty. During these formative years, I learned to do everything by myself and take care of myself. Later on, when I became a mother, I reflected on these childhood moments; no one ever taught me how to take care of myself or pampered me. There was no way my mom could as she had to raise eight kids. I feel in today's world, parents don't let their children learn and live or make mistakes. They want to create a perfect world, which in reality doesn't exist. I promised myself I would not do this with my daughter and raise her strong and with a mind of her own.

The Beginning of the Dream, Marriage and Motherhood

When I was growing up, I recall constantly thinking about a world where every person did exactly what they wanted to do, a world of total equality where there was no discrimination against a person because of their gender or ethnicity. Then I remember dreaming of travelling the world and having a career and an identity of my own. Utterly different to how I was raised.

I was always eager and the first one to put my hand up for any extra volunteering activity. I was a member of the Rotaract Club and compèred all the college events. From a young age, I loved being around people. I loved talking. (Unfortunately, I don't think I listened much even then!)

I longed for an identity of my own, not just as someone's daughter, wife, or daughter-in-law. I desperately wanted an identity all my own, independent of anyone else. I've always loved the idea of being on stage, inspiring other women with a message.

Then I got married.

I was given in marriage to my husband, a wonderful, supportive man and the centre of my life. I say "given" with no offence. I say this because I felt this was a choice that was made for me. If I had realised at the time that I had a choice, perhaps I may not have married at 21.

I never wanted to follow the family tradition, which meant being part of the family business or being a stay-at-home mom. I strongly desired to be a role model to my daughter and have a core identity of my own. As a teenager, I realised that my passion was people, and it was this same passion that led me to the recruitment industry. This is the best thing to have ever happened to me. I truly feel it was my destiny to be in the recruitment industry.

I've had the privilege of working with great organisations and had great mentors who have been instrumental in making me the woman I am today. This dream brought me to Singapore four years ago when I got a job opportunity, which has been another remarkable phase of my life.

Today I encourage my daughter to make her own choices and follow her dreams and live life. I encourage her to experience her life on her own first and to find out what makes her happy. Finding a life partner is beautiful, but it isn't the be-all and end-all of life. I feel this ideology permeates so many Indian households targeting girls – limiting and restricting them from living out their purpose.

Realising the Dream Career

I started my career when my daughter was five years old. I was part of the family business, yet at the same time, I longed to have a job of my own and be an independent woman.

In the process of my first job hunt, I was clueless about what kind of job I wanted. I was only driven by the vision of being in a position that allowed me to do what I loved best: being with people. I didn't have any hidden talents.

I landed a job in the recruitment industry. I still vividly remember the fear I felt when I told my in-laws I wanted to work, and while they didn't discourage me, they could not see the need for me to work. In their minds, they felt I needed to focus on raising my daughter.

Nonetheless, I started working. It was not easy to juggle being a housewife, a daughter-in-law, and a mother in a joint family. I was not just juggling responsibilities. I was managing biases and the expectation that a woman's sole duty was keeping her house running smoothly and efficiently. For me, having a job was not for monetary reasons; it was more to prove to myself that I could have a new identity completely different from what I had known my whole life.

I knew, however, very soon after I got into the recruitment profession that it was this exact role I wanted to pursue in my career. I loved the idea that everything was black or white; either you made your numbers or you didn't, which was the best part for me.

This space allowed me to be my best version. Following my gut and my intuition never went wrong for me. I continued to do well, soon becoming a top performer in my field. After a few months in the recruitment industry, I realised I wanted to be in sales and the company's front end. I knew that was where I could add the most value.

As I tell my colleagues, clients and friends, everyone I meet is either a candidate or a client. I feel so blessed to be in this position of touching so many people's lives daily. Every day I meet people from different industries, backgrounds and life experiences, and that's exactly what keeps me passionate about what I do and has helped me discover myself every day. One thing that always plays in my mind is how many other women are there like me out there?

I never imagined that at some point, because of this career I was so passionate about, I would be faced with a choice to leave India and my family. I never thought I would be given a unique opportunity just like men get to leave for greener career pastures while their wives would be left behind to take care of the house and the children. I reached a stage where I was given the opportunity to make my career dreams come true.

It was a big move for me to come to Singapore, where I faced many firsts. The first time living alone and only did things just for myself whereas, in India, I was always taking care of everyone else.

When I moved to Singapore, one of the first questions a Caucasian lady asked me was, "What made you move to Singapore?" And my reply was, "I'm not a trailing spouse, but my husband allowed me to move."

While I was saying this, the impact of what I just said hit me. I could have said that it was my choice to move. That's when I realised I had a choice to do exactly what I wanted to do.

In a larger way, it also made me reflect that this is the case for many Indian women; they don't know they have a choice. Their world revolves around their families, their husbands, and their children. While there is nothing intrinsically wrong with this, many live with the weight of unfulfilled dreams and wonder if this is all there is to life.

Simultaneously they are bombarded by Western ideals of independence from the many TV shows they perhaps watch, watching other women live out their dreams and being passionate about their lives; women who seem to have it all together.

But to make this life-changing decision, one needs courage and conviction that this is possible no matter the odds. You have to follow the dream for the dream to follow you. That's what I chose to do; to follow my dream no matter where it led me, no matter the circumstances I might face, no matter the challenges. I decided it was worth it. More importantly, I decided that "I" was worth it.

Living the Dream

I have reached a unique stage in my life where I feel I can impact and support other women by telling my story and encouraging them not to give up.

What seemed like a challenging and tough experience got me where I am today. It certainly wasn't a joy ride, but the journey was unforgettable, and now I live my purpose.

And most of all, I keep reminding myself – it's "my choice", and every woman can make her own choices. Dream it, wish it, do it.

About The Author

Lakshmi Murlidharan is a passionate, energetic, top-performing sales and consulting leader with over 18 years of recruitment experience within Recruitment Process Outsourcing, and Talent acquisition solutions. She has a strong track record of consulting sales and account management catering to "C" Level Executives globally.

She is well travelled and a fitness enthusiast and is always on the move. She strongly believes that "Happiness is when what you think, what you say and what you do are in harmony" and happiness is the highest form of fitness.

Lakshmi is a strong advocate for diversity & inclusion and front ends DEI initiatives through her current organisation. She is also an active member of the ENG women's leaders' group. She holds a postgraduate degree in Human Resources.

You can connect with Lakshmi at:

Email: *lakshmi.a.murli@gmail.com*

LinkedIn: *https://www.linkedin.com/in/lakshmi-murlidharan-1a445110/*

Facebook: *https://www.facebook.com/amu.murli/*

STORY THIRTEEN

Overcoming Barriers to Transform

I was transformed when I started to believe in myself.

"A reader lives a thousand lives before he dies. The man who never reads lives only one."

—George R.R. Martin

Today at sixty, reminiscing about my life, I ask myself..... "Was I a failure or a success by the world's standards? Have I lived my life to its fullest without any regrets? Was I happy with my dreams being on the back burner all these years?"

Coming from a small dusty village in the remote desert land of Rajasthan in India, I was the second child of seven brothers and sisters. Living with so many siblings was amazing. We loved, supported, cared for, valued and respected each other's wishes. We ate, played and watched each other's back. The best part was the moral and emotional support and loads of caring love. Being the eldest of three sisters I was the confidante, friend and mother figure.

However, in this arid land, there were no opportunities for any livelihood, so my father left to earn money to support his widowed mother and young siblings so they could have a better life at the very young age of eleven. He could barely read and write, but his willpower and discipline were indisputable.

It was from him that I learned the habit of reading and writing. I will always be deeply grateful to my father for bringing me to Chennai, a city in south India and enrolling me in a convent school. I don't know why he chose me. Perhaps he saw in me a spark or reflection of himself and he wanted to give me the education he had been denied due to his life circumstances. He was a girl-child supporter!

In those days, it was unheard of to educate a girl and even less so in a convent school. He transformed me from meek and silent into an independent, confident and extroverted girl. He even introduced me to the rich culture of Carnatic music and dance.

In school, I excelled in both studies and sports. I became the Games Captain and took part in quiz contests bringing fame and glory to my school. I was also selected to represent Chennai and got a scholarship from the state government. Life was awesome then.

Everything changed overnight when I got married at the very young age of 16. It was not unusual to be married at such a young age. With the average family having seven to ten children parents felt the need to settle their children, in particular their girls.

In those days they had to spend a huge amount of money for a girl's marriage. It used to take a lifetime for a father to fulfil his duty as a provider for his family. In my case, he saw in my husband a good man who would look after his daughter. But I was not ready to marry and settle down. Sadly in the Marwari community (to which I belong), a girl has no say.

After marriage, I moved back to Jaipur in Rajasthan. It was a colossal shock, both culturally and emotionally. My family was very conservative. Girls were conditioned from childhood to believe that their sole aim in life was to get married, look after their in-laws, have children and be a caretaker of their homes. Our heads had to be covered, and we had no say in anything. We could voice no opinions either for or against any matter. My extended family were very traditional and orthodox.

My husband's family, however, had a broader vision. My grandfather-in-law and my grandmother-in-law were trailblazers and very progressive in their thinking. It was due to her illness – she was in the last stages of cancer – that I was married very quickly. She was a woman of immense substance, courage and wisdom.

My husband was the apple of her eyes. She knew her end was near and she wouldn't survive much longer. Her last wish was to see her grandson married so she would give her blessings and the family heirlooms personally to the bride. She was immensely happy when we married.

I learned from her to not believe in superstitions and myths. In spite of all the hardships she faced in life she never ever complained. With all the pain she endured she was full of grit, courage, hope, tremendous strength and patience. She influenced me greatly and gave me the courage to go on when times were difficult.

As a young bride, I was ridiculed, taunted and put down for not having a professional degree. If you knew how to sew, knit and cook, you were deemed a good homemaker. But I was an exception to the rule.

My passion for reading and writing did not gel with everyone. I was looked down upon as an exotic insect that had lost its way. I was unlike the stereotypical perfect daughter-in-law. While the ladies of the house discussed making pickles, jams, knitting and other housewifely topics, my mind wandered, and I would think about what to read next or which book to buy.

I used to feel depressed and unhappy and became an introvert. I started to read in the bathroom or with the aid of a torch late at night. The silver lining was I had a loving husband and three beautiful children. Even while breastfeeding, a book was always in my hands. The hunger for reading never left me. My husband lovingly subscribed to a few good books for me, like *Reader's Digest.*

For 22 years, I focused on being a good daughter-in-law, wife and mother, fulfilling all my duties, taking care of my children's education, nursing family members with multiple sicknesses and post-operative care, cooking, serving, and doing laundry.

My life was rather boring and very tedious. Books and music were my lifelines. My family pushed me to try other avenues. I was always a person who took up challenges in life. I took things in my stride accepting the hardships that life threw me by balancing them with positivity knowing that one day I would fulfil my dreams.

My mother-in-law supported my grooming to be proficient in all matters. She even encouraged me to give a stage dance performance.

I dreaded going to parties and functions with my husband because the first question I was asked was, "What do you do?" I was ashamed to say I was a housewife as the rest of the women were in professions like doctors, engineers or business entrepreneurs. I never enjoyed these events, for I used to feel mortified, panicky and depressed. I eventually withdrew into my shell.

One day I said to myself, "Enough is enough. It's time for me to do something credible." I had excelled in my duties as a wife, mother, daughter-in-law, and now a mother-in-law, but the niggling ache was also there to write and, through my writing, become more and do more.

My father has always been my role model. When he was able to build a business empire without any formal schooling, then what was stopping me from achieving my dream of writing? With renewed purpose, I started reading more and grooming myself to be the writer of my dreams.

It's almost miraculous what a dose of self-confidence can do! I now could hold my ground and talk on any subject. People started complimenting me on my quick mind and intelligence. I was even asked from which university I had graduated!

The turning point in my life came in 2006 when the first Jaipur Literature Festival was held. It was bitterly cold and rainy, and the first day ended in a fiasco. It was a complete washout. The media didn't cover it because English events were not given any importance.

But the fire in me had been ignited. I was determined to attend the next one, and I did! What a feeling! I sat through all the sessions, transfixed and enthralled. I missed all my meals surviving on tea, revelling in the discussion and absorbing the talk on various topics and books. It was a very basic and rustic setup with many celebrities and a handful of audience members, but it was a life-changing experience for me.

The feeling was incredible. Now my vision was clear. I knew where my true interests lay. I would be that writer I had always wanted to be. I was on a high.

My passion for writing was ignited. It flowed like hot blood in my veins. Reading transported me to bygone eras, romances and wars, adventures and tragedies, revolutions and inventions, etc. I wanted to be a writer.

Now I want to live my dream of writing more than anything else. All the years of putting myself last and everyone else's needs before mine had to change.

I had to expand my boundaries and live more, do and experience more if I wanted to live my dream. I started reorganising my life and daily schedules.

When you become aligned to the Universe, the Universe starts working for you. Whoever I met started encouraging me to write, be it blogs, posts or articles. I thought, "Why not?" A start had to be made somewhere.

One day, a friend who had written and published a book said, "Nirmala, you can do it. Take action now." My faith and confidence grew as even my family started encouraging me.

The fire inside me was burning bright. Nothing was going to stop me. It was as if I had developed wings. I did not know how to type. I had never worked on a laptop. I wanted to cry. The submission date was looming. Throughout the night, I typed, and edited, knowing this time I had to win.

The other day I heard a keynote speech on Limiting Beliefs. This made me take a hard look at myself. It was an eye-opener.

The concept that "You are your very own limitation," touched the core of my heart. I contemplated it and realised it was true. So what if I had not completed my education? I had other strengths which I could easily tap into. But I created a prison for myself in my mind, creating and believing the stories of my self-limiting beliefs, wallowing in it had become my comfort zone. We all want to play small, and we tell stories to ourselves that become an impediment to our growth.

I overcame those self-limiting beliefs, and today I'm an international author. When I first held that book, my first book, in my hands, I cried and cried. It was as if I was holding a newborn baby.

I believe that even at 60-plus years old, there is still time for me. Maybe I don't have a degree, but I have raised a beautiful family who are well settled and have created names for themselves. I have raised my grandchildren with good ethics and manners, and are responsible little beings. I have the satisfaction that I have the experience, knowledge and wisdom.

Once I took that small step forward to live the life I wanted, all my insecurities, fears, and depression vanished. Yes, I was transformed when I started to believe in myself. I am still a work in progress. But, I feel cleansed of all negativities, negative impressions and conditions of the baggage I had carried all these years. Now that I am confident in my abilities and aware that I am as important as any man, I want to do things – learn and relearn, write more and fly high. I want there to be no barriers! I continue to read as often as possible, and there are more books to be written in my future!

What about you? What are the limiting beliefs that are holding you back? Have you been living with insecurities too?

As you read this, think that a new dawn has begun for you. This dawn will be full of hope, opportunities, love, forgiveness and gratitude.

Don't let anything or anyone stop you from achieving your dreams.

About The Author

Nirmala Singhee was born to transform people into leading happy, peaceful and joyous lives. Being empathetic and compassionate she excels as a social worker. Her vision in life is to contribute to women's empowerment, education of girls, saving nature and betterment of humanity. Her forte is counselling and helping the less fortunate, especially the deaf and mute.

Born in India, Nirmala lives in Jaipur, also known as the beautiful pink city, with her loving family. She did her schooling in Chennai and worked part-time in the family business. Nirmala's story is of grit and perseverance and how she rose against all odds to soar high. She likes to describe herself as a committed bibliophile, social worker, art aficionado, and an avid gardening enthusiast who holds a wanderlust close to her heart. She also loves to catch up with her friends and family over a cup of tea or coffee.

You can connect with Nirmala at:

Email: *nirmalasinghee@gmail.com*

Facebook: *https://www.facebook.com/nirmala.singhee*

Instagram: *https://www.instagram.com/nirmala_singhee/*

STORY FOURTEEN

Rebuilding from the Ashes

Be resilient, agile, flexible and move faster as we prepare for what is next.

I was blessed to be born on the southern tip of India, where three seas meet and time does not exist. My earliest childhood memories include growing up in my grandfather's house, listening to his words of wisdom and those of our forefathers and learning old-world values. I loved spending time on the rubber plantation, learning about spices and the tricks of my ancestral trade.

I remember my childhood with God-fearing parents and grandparents who treated everyone with respect and care. They provided opportunities. They saw good in everyone and everything. I am thankful.

We were blessed with hard-working friends and families running successful businesses. They believed in contributing positively to the community. We would travel 150 km to my paternal grandparent's place during the school holidays.

We were not fortunate to have the 'comforts' of modern society, such as uninterrupted electricity. We lived a life close to nature. I recall my time in nature, near the streams and ponds. I remember the taste of fresh food and creamy milk. Life was full of learning and experiencing the wonders of nature and good people.

During my school days, I knew I was different as I had challenges grasping some complex math concepts (e.g. analytical geometry). My parents supported my learning and arranged for an expert tutor who helped me overcome the issue. My love for learning was formed as I was curious. I loved learning and spent a lot of time understanding in-depth concepts. I was curious about learning the trade. I spent a lot of time with our neighbours (a family of very successful business people).

I wanted to help everyone and make the world a better place. My initial career choice was to be a doctor. This dream was crushed when I couldn't get into medical school. I chose instead to become an engineer (my Plan B), inspired by my uncle, whom I admired greatly.

My parents enrolled me in an engineering school in a village 200 km away from home. I was away from home for an extended period for the first time. Here at this engineering school, I got to know the real me. The world that I believed in (where everyone was equal) collapsed. My values were questioned, and I realised being a woman in India had its own challenges. I couldn't go to the shops alone, travel, or do anything independently. Women were expected to have a male escort (usually a father or a brother).

I decided to challenge this norm and live on my own independently. This was, for me, a life-changing experience. Living alone (as a girl) was a rare thing, but it gave me the freedom to experience and do what I wanted, to choose a life beyond constraints and make my path. I used the time to publish papers, giving me access to students and cohorts from other universities. I learned to dig deeper and find strength and embrace every opportunity.

During my final year of engineering studies, I realised my heart was in business, and I decided to pursue a master's in business administration. I was selected to attend a traditional (value-based) business school where I had the opportunity to learn from the best. The professors were ahead of their time and inspired us to be our best selves. I capitalised on every moment and worked on projects with different cohorts, collaborating with possible business schools and industry experts. Unfortunately, I lost my maternal grandfather and, shortly after, my paternal grandmother, who had a lasting impact on my life.

I had to face my fear of getting married, a tradition and expectation in my culture. To escape my fear temporarily, I found a job as a trainee in a logistics company that paid less than the minimum wage. It was tough during the Y2K scare. I was one of three women in a group with over 10,000 male employees. One of my female colleagues and I became best friends, and together we learned to look beyond constraints and experience what is possible. This brought a lot of perspectives, and I was blessed to receive such knowledge, real-life experiences and true friendships.

A year later, I had an opportunity to become an SAP consultant for an American organisation 700 km away. I packed my bags and moved to Bangalore. It changed my life. The role was exciting. I trained hard and worked hard. The following year I got to work in very remote locations in the sub-continent. I also got married (as was the tradition), another life-changing event.

The marriage did not turn out as I expected. I had a few warning signs after the engagement ceremony, but I did not dare cancel the wedding because I feared society and the potential shame to my parents.

I went ahead with the marriage with a heavy heart and a hope for things to turn out better. My fears were realised, and things took a turn for the worse. A week after the marriage, he started hitting and insulting me, calling me names. I didn't tell my parents or anyone else as I was ashamed. One day he hit me so badly that I was left unconscious. He called his dad, who advised him to leave the house. I remember waking up and calling my dad for help. My broken-hearted dad turned up on my doorstep after an arduous 12-hour bus ride.

As was the tradition, my dad discussed the situation with my ex-husband's dad (who didn't seem to have a problem with the event), and the parents agreed that we continue to stay together. My mom and dad took turns living with us to keep the peace. When my mom was living with us, my husband got angry and hit both my mom and me.

This triggered a thought in my brain which had not occurred before. As I lay hurt, I realised that this marriage was not worth it for the sake of society. This laid the foundation for the next set of events.

Thankfully, that same week I received an offer to work in the US, which I accepted. I packed my bags and informed everyone I was going on a short trip. The night before I left, my ex-husband beat me so badly that my eyes and forehead were swollen.

When he was hitting me, he told me that he would hurt my parents (who were sleeping in the other room of the apartment) if I screamed for help. This became the turning point for me, and I decided I would no longer live with this monster. The safest thing to do was get my parents out of the house and figure out my next steps.

The next day, just before I got on the plane, I shared the previous night's events with my dad. My dad had suspected something as my eyes were visibly swollen. He asked me if I was ok to travel and gave me some Indian rupees. I changed these to US dollars at the airport and got on the plane. That was the end of my life in India.

The events after this shocked me even more. I finally decided to separate and file for divorce. Everyone was against it (except my dad). My mom was scared of society's opinion. I cannot count the amount of shame, threats and criticism my dad had to endure to support my decision. After many prayers, my dad and I embarked on a six-year legal battle for divorce. My dad and I faced shame in every possible way. Society then could not understand, and we became the object of ridicule.

Everyone saw me as a successful professional who did not conform to the ways of society. With every legal hearing, my dad and I endured numerous insults from everyone around us. After multiple hearings, the judge finally decided that I was telling the truth and granted the divorce. This was one of the hardest battles of my life.

Many days I went without food (divorce was expensive) and did a lot of couch surfing and other crazy things. I learned a lot of valuable lessons that money cannot buy.

These events proved that we could sail through the storms with faith, determination, strength and courage. I have lost many friends and relatives in the process, but gained many new friends from unexpected places, gained strength in ways we cannot imagine, and challenged my beliefs in every possible way. The experience helped me see the good in everyone and every relationship.

I was one of those impacted by the Global Financial Crisis, but I couldn't return to India. Miraculously God gave me a job in Australia where I could start a new life. At 28, I promised myself I would embrace every opportunity and keep my loved ones safe. Since then, I have made Australia my home. I have worked with teams in more than 55 countries. I have lived in many places and enjoyed helping organisations undertake significant transformations.

Recently something stopped me in my tracks for which I had to pause to understand.

A trusted advisor asked me, "Do you feel you are treated differently because you are different?". The simple answer is, "Yes". Having lived in a male-dominated society for the majority of my life and working for years in a male-dominated environment, being a woman requires a lot of courage.

After pondering on this deeply, I believe that we as women would experience this at some point in our lives. Most of us would have developed superior masking techniques or would have broken this barrier in different ways. Here are some of my learnings.

- We have learned to work harder and be smarter than everyone in the room to be heard. We make humility our advantage and remind ourselves that we are created for a purpose beyond ourselves.
- We actively work on breaking down barriers and strive to leave a better and kinder world for the younger generations. We choose to capitalise on the investments our pioneers have made. We understand everyone has a different journey and will play our part in making the world more inclusive.
- We would have fought our fights, developed the needed skills and worked very hard to have a seat at the table and be paid the same as our male counterparts. We will remember that every uphill climb is worth it as we make a better world. We actively remind ourselves that we are stronger than our daily criticisms. We see beyond our limitations and will use every learning to our advantage.

Ultimately, we have gained valuable experiences and made life-long friendships that stand the test of time or any other barriers. Silent spotters, cheerleaders and friends represent these gains. We have learned to trust those around us, the data and our intuition to make evidence-based decisions. We have learned to be resilient, agile, flexible and move faster as we prepare for what is next. Above all, we have experienced that the world is a genuinely fantastic place filled with people who continue to break the norm.

Ultimately my advice to you is:

- Follow your heart; it is who you are!
- Change is a part of life, and it comes in many forms. In most cases it comes in difficult circumstances, trying times and in ways we least expect. Remember who you are, your values and your foundation. Change helps you evolve and prepare for the next stage in life. Change transforms.
- God always has a plan, a plan much higher than ours. It's our duty to do our part. For some of us, it means breaking the barriers and forging a way forward for many to follow.

With this advice, you can overcome and achieve anything.

About The Author

Judith O'Callaghan is a passionate technology-focused senior business leader whose mission is to leave a legacy of effective decision-making and building functional and innovative (high-performing) teams that deliver industry-leading outcomes, which will make the world a better place.

Judith began her career in logistics in South India, where she grew up. She relocated to the United States in her early 20s and then to Australia, and the rich tapestry of experiences that Judith has gained from living and working on three continents is invaluable.

Judith's journey in the IT industry has been interesting and she has delivered more than 500 projects throughout her career but now enjoys working as a specialist Program Director and Practice Lead, inspiring global teams.

Judith enjoys spending time with the people that she loves, and time outdoors in nature. Her interests include travelling and ancient history.

You can connect with Judith at:

Email: *judith.karunaharan@gmail.com*

LinkedIn: *https://www.linkedin.com/in/judith-o-callaghan-05a9bb13/*

STORY FIFTEEN

Self Love

Be brave enough to help yourself,
for yourself and no one else.

Have you ever felt like changing yourself?

You know you need to be more sociable. You know you can't live alone on an isolated island. You know you need to learn to talk. You know you have a lot to break through.

But then you are reluctant to be another person who is not you. You hated your old self. But you also hated the "changed" self. You kept dancing between the new you and the old you and reached nowhere.

By now, you would have asked me, "Amye, so what do we need to do? Change ourselves or be our old selves? I am so confused!!!"

I would say, "Just be yourself by first knowing who you really are, who you really want to be, and where you want to go".

Sounds simple, but it is never easy. Until you've experienced this process, you won't fully understand the meaning and the feeling behind the power of understanding yourself, being yourself, and showing up for yourself.

I have transformed from a person who didn't smile much, who didn't talk much and when I did speak every word was filled with negativity.

People around me now love my smile, my positivity and my insights into life. I always get comments like: I love your smile. I love your positivity. I love your posts on social media – so positive and inspiring.

But, do you know that I have hated myself since I was young? Yes. I really did. I didn't even like my name, my surname especially. This is because, for Chinese, our surname represents our father. And since young, I've had the impression he left the family because of me.

Looking into the mirror? Don't even mention that. I was totally disinterested in looking at myself in the mirror.

I didn't like to talk as I labelled myself as a person with a "laser mouth". I was super great at hurting people with words.

I love being alone and at the same time love to mingle with people but without talking. My role in any outing was just to nod my head and smile.

Even my smile wasn't genuine as it was filled with fear. In my head, there were always many voices and constant self-talk.

"Do I look good smiling like this?"

"What will they think of me if I answer that way?"

"I think if I answer that way, they will reply with this, this and this".

By the time I had imagined the whole scene, the conversation had ended. I didn't even have the chance to reply.

My next step was to beat myself up, to scold myself in my heart.

"How useless are you? You didn't even know how to open your mouth and say something at your age! You looked so silly! You looked like an idiot!"

Whatever harsh words you could think of, I had used them on myself. Whatever awful names you can think of, I definitely had called myself them before!

Can you imagine having someone so negative, so demoralising, so unsupportive living inside you for more than three decades?

Can you imagine how suffocating it was?

Since I was a teenager, I had thought of looking for help from a psychologist. I really had the intention to seek help. But I had no money. I was so young. And I just left my problem as it was.

Stepping into working adult life, I still had the same problem. I couldn't express myself properly. I didn't trust anyone including myself. I pushed myself hard telling myself I must excel in anything I do. I couldn't let anyone know about my weaknesses. I was the tough one and the great one in anyone's eyes. Family, friends, colleagues and bosses. I kept seeing the great people around me and told myself to be like them. I changed to be like them. But deep inside me, I didn't like the me I had changed into. I didn't like the feeling of being with others. I didn't like the feeling of wearing a mask. I just didn't like the "new" me at all. I started to hate myself. I didn't know my true identity. I was just a mix of rubbish!

I accumulated all these rubbish thoughts over the years, bringing them along with me anywhere I went, and in whatever I did. I, at last, broke down. I collapsed, filled with frustration, self-hate, guilt, and lots of confusion. My mind was tangled into a mess, to the level I couldn't untangle it on my own.

Here was where I started to think of ending my life. This was an easy way out. I sort of had thought about it a few times. Twice to be specific. I had tried to take action but didn't do it.

Speeding consciously (knowing the danger but accelerating anyway) during rainy days, my car skidded and just slightly hit the ramp of a highway. A failed suicide attempt!

I accelerated my car even though I knew I was close to the toll booth. I felt like ramming the booth and that's it. See you in the next life.

I am so glad now that I failed.

My ego, my so-called toughness, had cost me a fortune. Not monetarily but in my mental well-being, my relationship with mom and family members, the way I worked for others and with others, the relationship with myself and my friends, and so much more.

I had forced myself to be a person who was not me. I didn't love myself at all. I didn't have close relationships with my mom, sister and cousins. I didn't share my unhappiness with them, not even all my happiness. I was a loner. This took a toll on my health.

The unreleased anxiety and feelings, whether it was happiness or sadness, caused me to have serious eczema all over my arms, hands, fingers, body, legs, and toes.

I was already a person with low confidence and self-esteem. This incident caused me to drop into a deep valley in my life. I wore long sleeves, and long pants all the time even when the weather forecast predicted 35 degrees Celsius. Friends and colleagues always asked the same question: "Don't you feel hot?" Passers-by looked at me strangely. I immersed myself in work to forget about all the feelings I had in me.

Because I didn't talk much, I became unable to make any decisions. I couldn't decide what to eat, where to go for a holiday, what the next step was in a project, or how to handle conflicts among colleagues. I was afraid that doing it one way would hurt the other party. I didn't stand up for my colleagues and always just received orders from the management. All these behaviours were hard on my colleagues, me and unexpectedly on my mom and family members too.

I never liked being at home. I didn't want to face my family members. I didn't want to create happy moments and memories with them because I was so afraid I would lose them one day and I wouldn't be able to cope with the grief. I chose to put my career at the top of my priority list, followed by friends and my family coming into the picture as a third priority.

I lost so much of my childhood, my life as a student, my life as a daughter, my life as a sister and my life as someone I wanted to be.

You would probably be thinking by now. "Amye, since you spent most of your time at work, you must be very successful by now. Aren't you?"

Yes. I did achieve many things in my career. Because I was unable to be a good leader, not able to empathise with others, and not able to see things through the eyes of others, I only had I, me, and myself in whatever I did. I concluded that I was never successful at all.

I got projects done by pushing my team till they couldn't breathe. Because I worked overtime with them, they didn't reject me even when we needed to work till 4 am. Some of them even stayed overnight at the office (sleeping a couple of hours in the office) and continued to work after that. I myself went home, refreshed myself and went to work again. We really worked together and went all out.

Can you imagine how my colleagues felt? At that time, I didn't even consider how they felt. I only thought of the project. I didn't think about how I felt either.

I wonder now, how my colleagues at that time could stand my nonsense. Now I think back, I could see how horrible a manager I was. Cold-blooded, with no empathy, no social life but just work and work and work.

However, I am grateful that I was not stingy in sharing knowledge. At least my colleagues could still see some good in me. I really shared each and every single thing I knew without holding back.

Guess what! I didn't even realise how awfully I had treated my family, friends, colleagues and especially myself until I started my journey of transformation in 2021. I slowly realised how horrible a person I was previously.

I felt how they felt. I felt how I felt.

I reflected on so many situations in my life throughout 2021 and still continue this reflection while I write this chapter in June 2022.

So, what brought me to where I am today? How have I so suddenly (over about eight months), transformed into the positive and energetic me without hating myself anymore? It is so easy for me to tell my story and how I got out of my deep valley. But, it was never easy for me before and during the process of transformation. I am sure it will never be an easy thing for anyone who shares a similar story to me.

Back then, I was so lost in my life. I am grateful that I chose to find help online. I searched for information. Maybe because I searched so hard, a women's empowerment platform with three women entrepreneur coaches popped up on my social media.

Since a one-to-one session with one of the coaches, my life has never been the same. I followed their posts, and I went to their classes. This made me shift my mindset to positivity. I joined all the groups created for the online classes. I played full out. I did all the tasks I previously dared not to do. I pushed through all the ups and downs during the transformation process with support from the right communities.

With help, I got out of the deep valley in less than 12 months. All because I was aware of what I was going through without avoiding the issues. Being mindful of where my mind and heart took me and turned the wheel "just in time" when they were not aligned.

In brief, the eight steps below can guide you if you are experiencing a journey similar to mine.

1. Find help from those who have experienced it and transformed out of it.
2. Be vulnerable to slowly share your story without any bad feelings.
3. Learn to have congruence between your mind and your heart.
4. Play full out and participate in any workshops you choose to join.

5. Understand that loving yourself is not a selfish act.
6. Write a gratitude journal daily for 90 days.
7. Wear no black top for 21 days, take a selfie and share it with the community.
8. Most importantly, trust the process and trust your coach.

And all of the above sums up self-love to me.

"My life has never been the same again with self-love and by knowing who I am. Nothing is ever too late. Be brave enough to help yourself, for yourself and no one else"

About The Author

Amye Wong is a food technologist by profession. In 2021 she started sharing her stories by writing on social media platforms. She fell in love with writing and started the habit of writing there and then.

Be it through gratitude journaling, or sharing on social media feeds and stories, Amye learned to express her feelings, happiness, joy and even her unhappiness through words.

She hopes to help her readers to transform together, find their life purpose, and ultimately achieve the abundance that they want in life.

Amye has taken eight months to transform gradually from a person who totally lost hope in life to a person spreading the light around. And she is so glad she didn't stop there. She keeps finding her authentic self and keeps spreading light to people around her.

Amye wishes to hear from you, about you, and your stories to spread out more light!

You can connect with Amye at:

LinkedIn: *https://www.linkedin.com/in/AmyeWongmy/*

Facebook: *https://m.facebook.com/AmyeWongmy/*

Instagram: *https://www.instagram.com/AmyeWong.my/*

STORY SIXTEEN

The Power of Resilience and Re-Invention

Finding yourself when all seems lost.

Introduction

We all have many stories that define and make us who we are. What follows is one story that has made me who I am. It took me ten to fifteen years to talk about some of the events, and as I re-read it, I find it strange that I have been able to condense almost 40 years of my life into a few pages, and even a bit strange that I have been able to share something that is so deeply personal.

The event

Death comes to all of us, but when it is sudden, at a young age and with multiple ramifications, the pain is all the more.

My father's death was probably the most life-changing event I have faced. It left my mother, brother and me with hardly any money, anchorless and in the middle of an existential crisis. We had to shift countries, our lifestyles and overall expectations while dealing with the sorrow of not having someone we deeply loved with us.

For many years I felt aimless, unaware of who I was, what I wanted and my place in this world. Even today, I can identify characteristics of mine born from that event, such as my need for physical security and the inability to depend entirely on anyone. However, with time I realised that I, like all human beings, have this unique ability to recraft myself even as life seemed broken.

I was able to pick those broken pieces and slowly, with patience and determination, create something so much more robust and unique than I ever imagined myself capable of. Today I feel capable of handling anything.

The beginning

I spent the first 18 years of my life travelling and studying across several different African countries, the majority being in Nigeria and then Botswana. My father was a professor and someone who was well-read, well-spoken, and highly intelligent, forcing all of us to have engaging debates even at a very young age. My mother was a typical Indian housewife running behind her husband and children, always thinking about what was best for them. I can pick out moments from my youth, almost like a video reel stored in a memory box, in the library of my mind.

Some of the poignant moments include:

- Travelling in my father's red beetle car in Nigeria while breathlessly watching soldiers packed in a vehicle carrying massive guns – was it a coup, or had the President been jailed?
- Living in an era of apartheid in Botswana and then watching the glorious release of Nelson Mandela.
- Having lunch and dinner with the family surrounded by my friends of multiple nationalities – Nigerian, Ghanaian, and Indian.

- Playing with my dogs and several cats and fighting with my mother over my need to keep all the stray animals I found.

I knew my life was different because I never did quite fit anywhere. All my expatriate friends and I would discuss it. We called ourselves residents of "no man's land". We just didn't know where we belonged.

The breaking

Botswana was a quiet sleepy place, as it bordered South Africa and we would watch the events taking place there with interest and sometimes trepidation. Racism was talked about a lot but it was like a debate and it didn't affect us at a personal level. We were all pretty secure and comfortable.

When apartheid ended, there was an opening of the borders and a massive rise in crime as those who were suppressed started asking for more and wanted an immediate change in their status. We heard that some of these crimes started trickling to the bordering countries.

Oblivious to all this, I had most of my life charted out, at least as much as a teenager can have...go to the US, work in journalism or activism. I spent a lot of time fighting with my parents as I wanted to leave and study abroad, and they felt I should wait. Money and career were not something I was bothered about. That was till everything unravelled. One day as I sat at home watching TV, I heard a strange noise.

I stood up to see my father pushing our front door, trying to close it. He was quickly overpowered, and a group of six or seven men jumped into the room and started beating him. I don't know how or when, but my mother was also lying on the floor. I stood there immobilised and suddenly felt a cold gun barrel on my throat with a man saying, "I am going to fuck you if you don't show me where your money is"

I started walking, and somehow I ended up in the master bedroom. My mind was jumping all over the place with no clarity. I had no idea where the money was or what I was supposed to do. I turned around and saw my father. He had blood on his vest, and my mother was behind him. They asked us to lie on the floor and said, "We will kill you if you look at us."

I thought about pressing our security alarm but realised it could lead to more problems and didn't want to take any risk that would jeopardise our situation.

The next couple of hours were harrowing as we didn't know who would come out of this alive. Ultimately, they just wanted cash, alcohol and food, and when they got them, they locked us in the toilet and left. We all hugged each other in glee. We were alive, and that was all that mattered.

However, several months after this incident, my father came home one day complaining of a stomach ache and left for the hospital. That was the last I saw him walking or alive again. He died of secondary-stage cancer, probably aggravated by this incident.

And then they were broken more

My mother wanted to move back to India, and despite the resistance from my brother and me, her decision prevailed. We moved to a small town in Kerala, India leaving our education mid-way with no clarity of what we would do next and the fear of not having any money.

I hated moving to India. I felt cheated. The life promised to me was taken away. I wanted to study in the US, and here I was, with no idea of whether I would even get into university.

Soon we became the talk of the area, given how we came back to India and the overall mindset of the small Indian town. I would sometimes see kids whispering about me. Strangers would stop me and ask me whether we had sufficient finances since no one in our family was working.

I would often question whether I was a bad daughter or maybe it was my fault in some other way. Today it sounds illogical, but at that time, I couldn't take my mind away from the many possibilities. I would also have a recurring dream of being attacked with my dad somewhere in the background. Or he would come back, and we were looking for a cure for his cancer.

It was a dark place to be in – with no money and limited support.

My mother soon started pressuring me to get married. She felt she needed to take care of that responsibility before our money ran out. I felt myself changing from the confident girl to someone I couldn't recognise. I was frustrated and often had nightmares of being attacked – a caged bird waiting to escape.

Somewhere in all that, I decided I would not live like this and had to escape. I can't say that I made the right plan, but I made a plan and just stayed silent going through the transactions every day.

However, I would think about where I wanted to be and I focused on financial stability as my end goal.

Putting the pieces together

Today, I think that emotion helped me take decisive action regarding my career and financial independence. I initially joined a college two years behind the rest of my class. I put aside all my fanciful thoughts and regrets and decided I would take one step at a time and focus on what I had at hand. I took the old me and leveraged it.

So, I went on to do my MBA with almost no money. As my degree ended, I realised what I wanted to do. I was determined to work. I searched for the right job, rejecting the jobs I got from the college campus. I quickly realised I needed to sustain myself and took the first decent job I got. It wasn't easy, but I felt my background gave me the perseverance I needed to keep going. Today, apart from

6 months of maternity break, I have never been without a job.

I did well in the corporate setting as I was quick to understand and collaborate with people, solve complex problems while seeing things from another person's perspective, irrespective of how different they were to me. All of this made me a natural in the consulting world. And, of course, it paid well.

I was also aided by a fantastic nanny and a supportive ecosystem of a husband, (who was also my classmate), mother and in-laws, who had all by then, given in to my needs.

Despite having a young child, I would put up my hand for all those complex, challenging projects, working in male-dominated remote areas.I found my background helped me establish my equality and get the job done despite the many roadblocks.

One of my highlights was when my client, a CEO in India, said, "Radhika, most women wouldn't see the need to work the way you do. I am so amazed at how you are sitting in our factory... and would really like my daughter to talk to you...". I finally felt that I had built my identity and proven to myself that I could rise. I had taken my sorrow and turned it into an ambition to succeed.

I often tell my husband that I don't need his money. He used to initially get irritated by it, but now understands (I think) that it just a way for me to establish my identity and is representative of what I went through in my life.

My life lessons

1. **Never give up** – have your dreams and keep at them. If it all seems too big, take one step at a time, but keep walking. Whenever I am in a difficult situation, I think about the attack and what I went through and I tell myself to stay the course. Sometimes when you are in a storm the only way out is through it.
2. **Always be financially independent.** This is key for all women, and it is non-negotiable. With financial independence comes a great deal of power. You suddenly have choices you could have never had before.
3. **Time heals.** Whenever I am upset over anything, I just give myself time. I have found time gives me clarity and perspective on everything. I say, I won't think about this for a week and see how I feel.
4. **Be self-dependent and self-aware.** It would help if you were your closest friend and ally, so be careful what you say to yourself. You need to be your greatest motivator, and you can be that only if you understand your strengths and rely on them to catapult you.

I can think about my past and the growth I have had with objectivity, analysing my actions, which is the beauty of hindsight. However, I also see myself as a work in progress, continuously learning and relearning.

About The Author

Radhika Unni is a Managing Director with Accenture with over 20 years of experience working with clients driving large-scale transformation. She is very passionate about the intersection of business and technology in solving problems and changing lives.

She has travelled extensively and has lived for almost half her life in various countries in Africa. She acknowledges that part of her life that has moulded who she is today and her belief in diversity, equality and inclusion.

Radhika believes that life is all about experiences and moments of joy so never says, "no" to an adventure or to trying new things.

You can connect with Radhika at:

Email: *radhikaunni@yahoo.com*

LinkedIn: *https://www.linkedin.com/in/radhika-unni-singapore/*

STORY SEVENTEEN

Walking the Path of a Career Pivot

Set your intention on where you want to go.

2020 was the year of the COVID-19 pandemic, when everyone's life, home and career were turned topsy-turvy. Living with an unknown caused havoc and gave blessings in how the pandemic played out for everyone.

As a digital marketer, I embraced this change quickly. I effectively moved to working from home and functioning in a digital environment which I was already used to since I had worked in an agile environment. But, never would I know by the end of that challenging year, my life and career would be turned topsy-turvy too.

My role was to run marketing campaigns to drive growth for general insurance products, of which the main business was travel insurance, a segment hit hard during the pandemic. Travel campaigns dried up, and other areas of businesses could not sustain this cash cow.

My role was made redundant, and I was put out into the employment wilderness at the pandemic's peak. Borders were closed, and people's lives were severely affected. I was one of the tens of thousands. Being thrown out of my safety net during the pandemic was not something I was prepared for.

On top of this, my dearest family members – my aged parents – were confined to their homes in another country. Their well-being was at the top of my mind. I was worried about their health because of the ongoing pandemic. I had a heavy heart, and there was tremendous pressure on me at this time. This was the biggest test life had thrown at me so far. How could I overcome this hurdle to pivot to my next career?

The saying goes, "When life gives you lemons, make lemonade." That was the mode I used in facing this adversity. When one is pressured hardest, that's when (surprisingly) the enigma of survival instincts kicks in! I had to get back up. There was no wallowing in the doldrums. It was up to me, myself and I. I am accountable for myself and have a responsibility to my aged parents.

I cannot let them or myself down! The survival instinct inside me stirred, kicked to the surface and propelled me forward. I had been through other difficult experiences in my career; I survived my first career pivot, which was tough, but I made it! That gave me the ammunition to move ahead with an incredible ferocity of focus and determination so that I could rise back up. I looked back and took hold of the positivity of my first successful career pivot. That gave me a much greater motivation to achieve this time. For my second pivot, I was much wiser, much better.

One of my strengths is that I am a strong planner and strategist. With my years of marketing exposure, strategising and planning my goals come almost as second nature to me. I work out my marketing goals and then plan, execute and measure their returns. And I take pride in running my marketing plans and my achievements.

This is a valuable skill set when focusing on goals especially going for a second career pivot at any time, let alone during a pandemic.

I mapped out monthly, weekly and daily plans. What are my targets? When do I need to take action? Who to connect with, where to focus and how to manage my time. And I kept repeating this.

It was my own "transformation" agile sprint. At the end of each week and month, I reviewed my progress. If things were not working well towards my goals, I modified my strategies and implemented new goals. I kept working at it to get better opportunities and responses to moving toward my career goals. I wanted to pivot into a sector other than insurance, and finance was my next career pivot.

Throughout this time, I had opportunities and met lots of people. While I loved engaging with others and meeting new people, it was draining as the process was becoming drawn out due to the pandemic. Good opportunities were scarce, and many a time, things came to nothing. I was even ghosted. The scale was tipped in the employers' favour then.

As time passed, the apprehension of the long-drawn process started to weigh on me. That was when I decided to change my strategy to upskill in data analytics and Python coding to hone my technical capabilities. I made full use of my time to build up my skills in these critical areas so that I would be future-ready for work.

I finally took up the challenge to learn to code! Oh boy, was I in for a surprise! It was a beneficial course, but the technical aspect of coding was a steep learning curve for me.

The course was full-time, meaning I had to spend extra hours revising Python coding as I was someone with a non-technical background. What had I gotten myself into? I was stretched to the limit in finding my next career pivot and studying full-time! It was a trying time.

Nights were spent staring at a black screen filled with codes and trying to make sense of it; my eyes teared from overstraining. Never before had I cried while studying. With Python coding, I sure did!! On top of that, I needed to keep on searching for my next career pivot.

I was running like an Energizer bunny, buzzing continuously from chasing career opportunities while studying my data and coding course. My inner drive and energy were buzzing so high that I worked on the all-time high drive of resilience and perseverance. I was absolutely charged to the maximum on wanting to achieve my goals.

Since my brain was constantly working, I had no time to think negatively. I was wired for continual growth and *Go, Go, Go*! It was not just my innate inner strength but also my strong mindset supported by the daily practice of meditation.

Vipassana meditation and yoga kept me centred and grounded throughout my challenges. These practices have been with me over the years and brought me great joy and strength to have a good balance of mind, body and soul. Tapping into them kept me going.

My next test was a golden opportunity that came through after a three-month interview process – the opportunity I was looking for in the finance industry. Yay! My hard work was bearing fruit, and my career pivot was happening sooner than I thought!

Nay, I was wrong. The negotiations for the opportunity went on and on like the interview process. It was a delicate balance of the option on hand versus my value. How much was I willing to give to accept the opportunity? I was hard-pressed to provide a lot more.

It became like a game of chess, with both sides waiting for each to make a move. Eventually, it ended in a stalemate and winless for both sides. After so much time and effort spent on both sides, an opportunity had come and gone.

That was a bitter pill to swallow. It was like I had gone on an exhilarating roller coaster ride and came back down with a crash landing. This was extremely hard to get over (then). It put a dent into my spirit, and I questioned what I was going through in finding my next career step.

Do you know what I did next? I did the best thing that I could. I gave myself a break. Not with a KitKat but with myself by taking a much-needed rest to reset.

After the rest, I reflected. I asked myself, was it a wise move? Did I forgo more than I could afford to let go of?

No, I did not. I was willing to stand up for what I believed my value was and did not regret my decision. I learned never to sell myself short and live with no regrets. I also decided to let go and give myself more time to move toward my career pivot. I was pushing too hard, wanting to win too fast. I needed to let things flow and be open to receiving.

There is a saying that "to receive, one needs to give". During my career pivoting journey, I gave in areas I found meaningful by mentoring, coaching and volunteering. I was helping others needing advice. I also increased my speaking voice by becoming an "I am Remarkable" trainer to train others on self-promotion, something I strongly believe in. I even conducted my first workshop for my coursemates.

I gave and watched others bloom and move forward. In turn, it helped me build a stronger foundation for myself and the belief that I could move toward my career goals. I received the positivity and joy of others that fed my inner strength further.

With persistence and grit, after six months of an intense roller coaster ride, the right opportunity finally came to me, and I pivoted into a marketing career in the finance industry. Amazingly, I hit my second career pivot within a shorter time frame than my first pivot and during a pandemic too!

It shows how a strong belief and innate determination drove me toward my goal. This time, I was more ready and flexible to change. My new adventure began, and I restarted my journey in my second career pivot in 2021.

Reflecting on my second career pivot, I realised other essential factors that I had capitalised on besides focusing on my strengths and setting targets. One of them was that I sought out mentors and advisors for guidance. This is a crucial factor in anyone's success. I had excellent career mentors that were my north star during the rollercoaster ride. They helped me improve and overcome my setbacks. Thus, I believe in the power of mentoring. I also had support from my coursemates and attended insightful talks that taught me to think outside the box. I learned that you need to build a robust support system to move forwards.

If you want to go far, go together. In getting to my next career pivot, I also leveraged my networking and connecting skills to build connections with diverse people. I sought out connections and asked for their advice. Connect and learn from the experts! Build on your networks continuously and sustain them authentically.

Keep learning and have a growth mindset. I took up learning data and coding, which was challenging. I may not be a super coder, but I have gained a deeper understanding and perspective on the applications. I learned new skills and broadened my knowledge. A continuous learning mindset builds a mindset constantly forging ahead, thus making it easier to adapt to career changes and pivots.

Lastly, being kind and cultivating proper self-care and mindset towards oneself is the best thing to adopt when going through a career pivot. Give yourself time to rest, relax and rejuvenate so you can keep moving forward and bounce back from setbacks. Focus on the positive and be grateful for the good around you.

Set your intention on where you want to go. Give out good vibes and energy. All these will put you in good stead in moving forward. You only have one YOU. Treasure and be thankful to yourself and the value of YOU. Know your worth and put your best foot forward. Taking one step at a time will eventually lead you to your chosen path. May you walk your best onwards.

About The Author

Valerie Chow has integrated marketing experience in both digital and offline environments, honed in retail through exposure to global brands from Nike, Marks and Spencer to Harvey Norman. She started her career in merchandising, evolving to branding and digital marketing.

The biggest "change" in her career was her first 180-degree pivot into the insurance industry, thrown into an agile working environment that needed a continuous growth mindset. Valerie's motto to keep developing led to her second career pivot into the finance industry.

She is a chameleon in career pivots and with her love to learn and grow, she has successfully reinvented herself with her drive and determination to push forward on new career frontiers.

This same motivation fires Valerie's passion for D&I and the leadership journey with her "I am Remarkable" training to empower others in building self-confidence.

This has led to her building her voice as a speaker and advocate for self-development for success.

You can connect with Valerie at:

Email: *contact.valeriechow@gmail.com*

LinkedIn: *https://www.linkedin.com/in/valeriechow/*

YouTube: *https://www.youtube.com/channel/UCCwKgHDUflrR64HfKXytf7g*

STORY EIGHTEEN

What does Life Want from Me?

Lessons on Paths (Not) Taken.

I was born and raised in a small town in The Netherlands, where I always felt a bit out of place. To me, it seemed everyone lived a relatively similar life which mostly took place in the same town. For as long as I can remember, I longed for more: to leave, explore and experience new things and live a different life than most people I grew up with. I don't remember ever dreaming of a particular career or profession. I just wanted to experience what life had to offer.

After high school, I first got a bachelor's degree in Communication in a city close to where I grew up. Then I ventured further out and signed up for a Master in Social Sciences in Amsterdam. Here, the city and university life offered me the new experiences I had been looking for: I moved into a student flat, signed up for a study trip to China (which was quite an exotic thing to do in those days), went skiing for the first time and made friends for life. My life in Amsterdam was like a dream come true, it felt like breaking free, and I couldn't have been happier.

I met my husband around this time. After several years together, he got an offer for a role in Switzerland at a large multinational company. I decided to join him and quit my first job as a Human Resources trainee, to jump into the unknown opportunity.

Our lives in Zurich ended when my husband moved to Germany for a new role, and I decided to return to

Amsterdam. I found a change management consultant job at a large international bank, and everything fell into place for the second time in my life. I loved my new job and colleagues and had total freedom during the week – my husband and I saw each other only during the weekends. During this time, my friends were buying houses and getting pregnant, but I didn't feel the urge to do the same. I even thought I could imagine our lives without having children. Little did I know.

At the end of 2009, I became pregnant. By then, I was more than ready and really looking forward to this new chapter in my life. It felt incredibly powerful carrying a baby and the standard pregnancy checks confirmed the baby and I were doing very well. Around 36 weeks of pregnancy I was about to start my maternity leave. The day before it started, my husband and I had an appointment with the midwife for a routine check. That check forever changed our lives; during the echocardiogram, the screen remained black, and the midwife could not find a heartbeat. After rushing to the hospital, our worst fears were confirmed: our little son had died in my womb.

From that moment on, things weren't the same. I struggled with many things triggered by our loss, and I remember there were days I hated the fact that I woke up at all. Never could I have imagined how much pain I had to endure; the grief was too much to bear at times. And still, I realised somewhere deep down that I would also learn from this experience, that I would come out stronger because for as long as I can remember, I have never been afraid to look life in the face. So I allowed myself to grieve, be angry, feel sorry for myself and ask the obvious question: why me?

Over time I learned this was not about me, that these things, however awful, happen and that this is also part of life. I learned about acceptance and the need just to keep moving on. Looking back, above all, I learned things *do* change for the better, even if very slowly. How you deal with this process and what you can learn from it makes the difference in the end.

After a period of deep grief and a stressful second pregnancy, our beautiful daughter was born. I was completely in love, and from that day onwards, I could leave a big chunk of pain and sorrow behind; she healed me in a way. I returned to work in a leading role for a large transformation programme at the bank and slowly found the right balance in my life. I loved being back in the workforce and also really enjoyed family life.

The years that followed were happy ones. I became pregnant again and, at the same time, was offered a role leading a large department, and I went for it. I loved this role; it was not easy, but I enjoyed the dynamics and learned so much about my leadership skills. I gave birth to my second child, a boy and returned to work again, juggling all the balls young mothers have to juggle. But at the same time, I was very happy and felt blessed.

Things suddenly changed when I discovered I was pregnant again, unexpectedly. My youngest was only nine months old, and my first thoughts were: this is too soon, too much to handle. My husband was still pursuing an international career, and I felt there was much more to explore for me at the bank. Another baby would change our newfound balance.

My husband was clear from the start that this baby was more than welcome. I felt the same, but I also worried about the practical implications constantly. Since I became a mom, family responsibilities were always there. Eventually, I embraced the unexpected change and soon, another beautiful son was born.

At this time, my older son's behaviour at home got worse and worse, with intense and frequent tantrums putting a strain on the family. We read many books on parenting, got advice from coaches, etc., trying to understand how to deal with our little boy. For a long time, we thought he just had to adapt to the fact there was a new baby in the house, but intuitively I knew there was more going on. We gave everything we had as parents, but it just wasn't enough, and it started to take a toll on us. Clearly, we had to make some difficult decisions as the situation could not go on like this.

We decided to leave Amsterdam and buy a house in a small town not far away. Leaving Amsterdam broke my heart; I wasn't ready to go, but I knew we had to for the family's sake and our son's. Of course, moving to a bigger house and getting a big backyard didn't solve our son's behaviour. It became even worse initially. We then realised we needed professional help and even medication to raise our child. It felt like we were failing as parents – but there was no alternative.

Work was a safe place and energised me at that time but home life was so challenging that it slowly drained me of all my energy, despite my intense love for my children. It was then that I was offered a new role, a promotion, again. I was very flattered and knew I could make a success out of this professional challenge but at the same time, I was utterly exhausted. I can vividly remember bursting into tears when speaking to my son's psychologist because I knew I was at such an important crossroads in my life. Deep down, though, I knew what choice to make. So I declined the job offer and decided to leave the bank, putting my corporate career on indefinite hold and focusing on my son, my family and myself.

I haven't taken up my corporate career since. Shortly after I stepped back, my husband was offered a role in Singapore, and we both felt this could be an exciting new chapter in our lives. We would be able to leave behind difficult years, our children would be able to attend a great school, and we could work on finding a new balance for the family. We were re-energised for the first six months, even though the family situation remained intense.

A balance of sorts emerged and new professional opportunities arose. Then COVID-19 hit the world, and instead of taking up new professional challenges, I ended up homeschooling three kids and feeling locked up. As for many others, every day felt like Groundhog Day, and our son was struggling to adjust to a world, as well as *his* world, gone crazy. I had now seen my equilibrium upended so often that I knew how to deal with this better than ever before: the situation was what it was, and there were still possibilities for me to create win-win situations.

I started coaching people in my network, became vice-president of a large charity organisation, signed up for an intensive certified international coach training and created and led a female leadership programme for an international female network organisation in Singapore.

The coach training became a significant journey and enabled me to reflect deeply on myself and my life. I realised that I didn't feel complete without having a career, that I didn't feel successful. I felt the pressure of meeting the expectations of others, but I now realised those were mostly my own expectations. I regularly thought of the many women that combined their careers with being a mom and asked myself why I wasn't capable of doing that. But I now knew the answer: my life story, like many women's, was not straightforward, and my specific circumstances were highly complicated. My story was that my son really needed (and still needs) me and I *wanted* to be there for him and my other two children. I had to plan my ambitions around this realisation, so I started doing just that.

I know I am not alone, that there are many women out there struggling in their own unique ways and on a path in life they did not, perhaps, actively choose. But I learned that you can make it *your* path and that a new balance can always be found.

Professionally, I learned that leadership is not limited to people having a "traditional" corporate career. I have learned much more about (female) leadership since I put my career on hold and experienced the rollercoaster ride of my life than ever before. I have experienced that I can make a difference as a leadership professional by supporting women (and men) that want to develop their leadership skills by helping them find a (new) balance in their lives, even in the face of professional and private challenges.

In the meantime, ever since we moved from Amsterdam, the intense family dynamic has remained and there are still moments I can't find the strength to deal with everything. But fortunately, those moments always pass. I try to embrace what I have, the good, the bad and the ugly and feel blessed about many things in my life – including my family.

From what I've seen and lived through, I know I will always be able to create a new balance and help others find theirs. To quote Eckhart Tolle: "*Instead of asking 'What I want from life?' a more powerful question is: 'What does life want from me?'*"

About The Author

Patricia Arkenbout was born and raised in The Netherlands and now lives and works in Singapore. She is a Leadership and Transformation expert and internationally certified coach with a passion to make a positive difference.

She particularly loves supporting women in their growth journeys and providing them with a mindset to deal with challenges as well as empowering them with courage and determination.

Patricia started her career in the financial services industry in a variety of senior leadership and transformation roles at international banks in The Netherlands and Switzerland.

Although she enjoyed her career and the dynamics of corporate life she decided to step back when combining her professional and family lives started to take a toll.

This decision forced her to make different choices in life, both professionally and personally and has been the driver of her interest in female leadership ever since.

You can connect with Patricia at:

Email: *p_arkenbout@hotmail.com*

Linkedin: *https://www.linkedin.com/in/patricia-arkenbout/*

STORY NINETEEN

What it Means to be Lost

Never underestimate the power of self-awareness.

I was one of those lucky baby girls. I had everything I wanted. I was loved and spoiled by my parents and grandparents. I had travelled almost half the world with my mom and dad as the only child in the first eight years of my life.

My life changed drastically moving into my teens. Whatever I wanted to have, was no longer a given. I had to think and work hard and smart to get what I needed the most, and even then, I sometimes did not get it.

This was when my parents went into bankruptcy for a decade or more!

During this dark period, I was moved out of a fancy private school to no school at all, leaving our luxury house in a main posh area to a rural one, and of course, getting bullied by so-called friends and physically abused.

This is when my grades fell, and I became an emotional eater and an aggressive unempathetic yet sensitive person due to the emotional and mental shock I experienced.

During this time, we had no money to buy food which meant minimal eating and mostly unhealthy, fattening food leading to obesity. I still remember the shock on my mom's face when she said, "Ghenwa! You ate the whole six burgers!!!!" It was traumatising for me. I ate them, not feeling what I was shovelling down my throat, accompanied with guilt because I could see my mom's distress at wondering what she would feed my younger sisters and dad. She was the only breadwinner for the family of six and earned a minimal salary.

There was no money to buy clothes which meant wearing the same clothes repeatedly and probably hand-me-downs. There were no new toys in line with the latest trends which meant borrowing other children's used toys. Yet, the most annoying thing was witnessing my parents fighting.

As we dropped social status, we witnessed many people walk away from our lives. This was when I started to lose trust in people. My belief in "***POWER IN ALL***" changed, as did my self-confidence. I devalued my worth and saw myself walking away from my dream every day. I started seeing myself as ugly.

While living through these drastic changes, including leaving school because I failed the government passing test, I had to pause, observe, and understand that this was my new life!

This is when I realised that I had to bring myself to the NOW… I had told myself that I have to be living in my present so I could start asking myself questions about how I should live to get myself back to where I wanted to be.

I started working in travel agencies as I had built experience from when my father had a travel agency. I studied it to increase my salary. I had the opportunity to attend evening classes in a run-down public school, and I passed my government exams after my sixth attempt!

Life then started working well for me because I changed my thinking.

I realised that ***what is meant to be, will be and shall be a blessed part of me!***

I kept studying and working hard. The years went by, and the time to join a reputable university was just around the corner.

Of course, my dream was to hit a top-tier university and major either in nutrition or fashion but unfortunately, it was not an option as my GPA qualified me for neither.

Again, I was pushed to make a rational decision based on the shortest study duration as I needed to find a well-paid job quickly, most affordable in terms of tuition fees, and most flexible in terms of attendance as I had to work more than 50% of my attendance time.

Even though my options were limited, and I found myself obliged to go to a tier-two university, I was grateful because majoring in Business Management opened many opportunities that helped shape the way I think.

I managed to join a wellness and nutrition centre, a booming industry back then. I embarked on this journey as their front-line customer service centre executive on the condition that I lose weight. I made a deal that "I become your guinea pig to prove to customers that the food and products of the business work well, and I will be a live and a real marketing tool for the business all at their expense."

Furthermore, I partnered with a children's camp during summertime, which I used to join over the summer weekends. This was the joy of my life because I had the opportunity to relive my missed teenage days. I used to enjoy playing with the kids, educating them on fashion and joining them at water parks.

I could have my younger sisters join at times, too, all at the expense of the summer camp deal. The deal was less pay for free food, free access to water parks, secured transportation and free access to my siblings.

This is where I learned that ***there is power in me!***

During my four years at university, I juggled between working and studying. Therefore, it was hard for me to pass courses all in one go. Luckily, our university had a program that supported working students by allowing them to fail four out of eight courses on the condition that we successfully passed the failed courses during summer or we had to repeat the whole year.

I used to study for four courses out of the eight in a year for the pre-summer exams and then refocus my energy on the remaining four I had to test for in summer.

As soon as I hit year four, I was informed that an environmental services corporation was hiring! I attended the interview and successfully joined their Human

Resources team. I had to continue juggling work and university, but this time it was more intense as I had to prove myself in a competitive corporate world.

After successfully passing my fourth year, my salary was adjusted. However, I was still paid less than others in my grade despite the same job description, simply because I studied at a tier two university.

However, I admit that what I learned contributed to the corporate woman and entrepreneur I am today.

Being underpaid was always a thorn in my side. I can't tolerate unfairness, but I can do something about it. Therefore, I have pushed myself to pave my way through the system and built a solid network just like neurons in the brain.

When the time came to move to the headquarters of the business unit I was serving, I never hesitated to take on this new and well-paid opportunity. Even though everyone said it was a risk, I saw opportunities, learnings, growth, and a future. I lived the belief that "*when you focus on possibilities, you will have more opportunities*".

I believed what I worked for and wished for would come to me in time. I learnt that ***I attract what I believe is right for me.***

Life at the headquarters was about challenges, acquisitions, projects, crazy deadlines, and business trips across the gulf region. Dealing with top management and being exposed felt like I was always on the go and always on the radar … but I loved it!

I loved it because it helped me come closer to my naïve dream of becoming a successful businesswoman in a red dress, stilettos, and a convertible car. Yes, this was it for me!!!

I enjoyed working under pressure, meeting new people, making new acquisitions, and living the start-up life across countries. On my last international project, which was Dubai based, I managed to relocate, settle, and lead a calmer life. I moved into a more back-office position which was also a form of a start-up for an internal HR function that required the designer in me to come to life. I felt more relaxed, and this is when I started questioning myself. Where am I today? Am I doing what I really like and want?

I call this ***the awakening***!

I started asking myself these questions because I felt I was stepping away from my dream. Therefore, I embarked on a self-development journey through coaching. I studied, got certified and started understanding myself more. I can tell you if you don't really know yourself, then you do not really know what you want to do and achieve for yourself in life.

I totally understand what it means to be lost! I advise you never to underestimate the power of self-awareness!

In my coaching journey, I discovered so many things about myself, such as my love of writing, my passion for fashion and design, and my love of sharing experiences which led me to jump-start my co-authoring journey in this volume, start up my fashion brand and allowed me to jump-start an e-talk-show during the COVID-19 pandemic at the company I work for today. Last but not least I was able to build my blog via Instagram to share my experiences in short epigrams and much more!

I learned to Trust the Universe!

When my job at the environmental services organisation was made redundant, I started doubting my talent and capability as some people also lost trust in my talent and potential. I questioned whether I was enough or would ever find a position where I could perform. I spent around four months doing a job search. Until one day, a leading American car manufacturer contacted me for an opportunity to join their HR Business Partner team. This was a nail in the neck for those who looked down at me.

The moral of my story is what goes around comes around. Preserve your energy for something that will come to you at the right time, and always pick your battles wisely.

I spent seven tremendous years learning, building international relations, making friends, launching an e-talk show, building my brand and reputation and much more until the awakening hour hit me again! This time it was a different kind of awakening. I felt empty!

I felt that something was missing. Reflecting on that feeling, I realised that the job I was currently doing was not entirely satisfying. This was when I decided to start working on my fashion dream. I started my fashion brand as a birthday gift to myself in celebration of entering my fourth decade.

I started it when I was financially broke. Yes, you can be financially broke at 40!

I worked day and night, and I am grateful for all my experiences. It is not easy to be an entrepreneur, but it is rewarding. My brand is a year old now, and I am taking it slowly as the saying goes "***Go Slow to Go Fast***"!

I have learned that ***where you are today is the sum of all the things that caught your attention and you acted upon in your past.***

Thinking about where I stand now in my corporate life, I believe I am not receiving what I really deserve regarding my growth and promotion. So the question is, what is next for me?

To everyone currently experiencing and struggling with setbacks and where they are unable to catch their dream or act upon it… I tell you this shall pass too because if I made it, so can you. Believe in yourself and you will rise too.

I have learned ***the journey of transformation starts with you taking that "Leap Of Faith."***

I know the term "Leap Of Faith" is cliché, but there is no better phrase than this to ignite confidence and call us humans to action.

There will be more to my story! You wait and see!

About The Author

Ghenwa Habbal was born and raised in Lebanon.

She is a well-rounded global HR/Talent Leader with over 15 years experience in strategising, designing, leading and delivering large-scale operational and talent initiatives.

Ghenwa is first a human, then a leadership coach, an epigrammatist, a strategic thinker, and a futurist as well as a strategic HR professional with experience across various industries and countries.

She is a passionate and strong advocate for Diversity, Equity, and Inclusion (DEI) and equal representation of genders across organisations. Ghenwa is focused on strategising, developing and retaining diverse talent and helping build an environment that cultivates inclusion and belonging whilst building capabilities and transforming organisations into talent factories.

You can connect with Ghenwa at:

Email: *ghenwa.habbal@gmail.com*

LinkedIn: *https://www.linkedin.com/in/ghenwa-habbal-b2874046/*

Instagram:*https://www.instagram.com/the_fashioned_hr_barista/*

STORY TWENTY

What Pandemic did to Us

And how grateful we are for it!

The Shaken

In December 2019, we started hearing about this strange virus that was making people sick in Wuhan, China. By January 2020, the virus had begun spreading to other countries and the first death due to the virus was reported. By the end of the month, the whole city of Wuhan was in lockdown and the World Health Organisation declared it a global emergency. Many of us here in Singapore thought it was an overreaction and perhaps not even as dangerous as SARS. The virus was given the name CoronaVirus, also known as COVID-19.

On 7th February, the Singapore government stepped up the risk assessment and introduced additional precautionary measures, even suggesting cancelling or postponing non-essential large-scale events.

It was a Friday night and we had an event at one of our most popular venues with over 250 attendees. The first question was whether we should cancel or go ahead. After much debate, we decided to go ahead, as it was too last minute to cancel. The hotel also ensured they had a system in place for us to carry out the required precautionary measures.

We printed declaration forms for attendees and carried out temperature screening. We pumped copious amounts of sanitiser on their hands, looked out for anyone exhibiting respiratory symptoms such as cough and runny nose, and even denied entry to some people who looked unwell. They weren't happy, of course! Lucky for us, our event went well with no one getting infected.

By March, the actual effects of the virus became even more prevalent, and countries started going into lockdowns. In Singapore, too, gatherings of more than ten people outside work and school were prohibited. This meant we had to cancel or postpone all our events. Frankly, we weren't fazed as we were confident that all of this would be over by summer and soon, things would go back to business as usual.

Within a month, things took a turn for the worse. The virus had begun spreading rampantly. Having young kids at home who are most vulnerable was highly worrisome. On 3rd April, Singapore announced a nationwide partial lockdown, also known as a circuit breaker, to contain the spread of COVID-19. Now the panic started to set in.

Everyone was advised to work from home. Kids, too, had to be home-schooled. There were crazy wars at the supermarket, with people fighting for toilet paper and essential groceries. Hand sanitisers and disinfectants were out of stock. People avoided interacting with each other in fear of being infected by the deadly disease and being transported to already overcrowded hospitals. No one knew what the real extent of this virus was.

As time progressed, there were no signs of restrictions easing out, and travel was completely shut down. During this time, we decided to make the most of it by spending quality time with the family, baking bread, making cocktails, and even coming up with our own version of the Olympic games in the house to keep the kids busy. I even started a YouTube channel for my kids with pretend videos of them travelling around the world, including using fake accents and meeting the Queen!

The Stirred

For a while, it seemed like fun, but then the reality started setting in. Whilst my Facebook posts showed I was having a great time, in actuality, I was struggling to keep it all together. None of us were used to being in an enclosed space together all the time. My home office was taken over by my husband having loud Zoom calls. Trying to home-school young kids and keep them entertained inside the home was becoming impossible. Despite domestic help, planning meals and snacks for the whole family was a stressful chore. Finding delivery slots for groceries was like winning a lottery. Given my (usually) very active social calendar, not being able to meet friends was very lonely. And the constant worry of aging parents and in-laws, living overseas was extremely stressful.

At first, I thought only I was going through these emotions. But when I spoke with my friends and other women in my network, I realised most of us were going through the same experience. Those who lived by themselves had it even worse. Overall mental health for women especially was at an all-time low.

Having been at the forefront of supporting and empowering women, I knew I had to do something about this. And that's where the idea of ***#MyVoice*** was born.

In June 2020, we (my business partner, Shikha and I) organised a small virtual event for women in our network to come together to talk about things that mattered to us, to discuss issues and challenges we were facing and to just be ourselves. We wanted to create a safe space where women could agree, disagree, or agree to disagree but without any judgement. The outcome of the event was astounding. What an impact one small event had created! This motivated us to do more.

We continued to host these free events every week to support women. Now with online events picking up, we had women from all over the world joining us to have an interactive discussion with subject matter experts to become better versions of themselves by listening, learning, helping, and supporting one another through this journey. In no time, our community grew to include thousands of women from across the globe.

Soon we realised the power women's voices had and how it is crucial in creating inclusive, open, and prosperous societies. We wanted millions of people to hear the authentic voices of women from our diverse and thriving community. This drove us to the idea of publishing their empowering and inspirational stories in a book to be titled

#MyVoice. In doing so we would celebrate exceptional accomplishments and achievements of everyday women around us.

Everyone we spoke with was thrilled to be part of this initiative and share their journey in the book. We started putting their stories together and reaching out to more women. Things were going great!

But then, we struck a real roadblock. Many of the publishing houses we contacted did not respond to our enquiries. For months we did not know if they had not had a chance to see our emails or whether we were flat-out rejected.

We finally sneaked our way into one of the well-known publishing houses and got a meeting. Here we found out that we wouldn't even be considered for a glance unless we had a literary agent! But the issue was that no literary agent was interested in representing us because most of our authors were first-time writers. We argued that if no one gives us a chance, we will always be first-timers! So, it became a bit of a chicken or egg situation.

After a lot of research, we came across other publishing houses willing to take on our project but at an extremely high cost and without committing to any marketing or promotions. At that point, we knew if we couldn't market our book, we would be lucky if even five friends or relatives of each author bought the book! And that would defy our entire objective in publishing these stories.

This wasn't even a roadblock. It felt like a dead end! All our work was wasted, and we felt like complete failures, especially knowing that we no longer would create the impact we wanted to.

By now, it was November 2020. I clearly remember the day. Shikha and I were sitting on the balcony at her house. I was on my third whisky when I suddenly jumped from my chair (almost freaking her dog out who was sitting on her lap) and said, "You know what? We are just going to do this ourselves."

"Do what ourselves?" Shikha asked.

"We are going to set up our own publishing house!" I exclaimed, gulping down my drink.

"How hard can it be?" Famous last words, as they say!

The Undeterred

The rest of the evening was a blur as we started to plan our next move. We soon realised it wasn't as simple as we thought. But with the guidance of my cousin, who had experience in publishing books, we had a publishing team together within a few weeks.

The best part was that our team worked virtually and spread across the globe. We had to deal with many time zones, but that was a minimal price to pay for the flexibility and cost savings. We even designed our logo and our first website on our own. It wasn't until we made some money that we got a professional one done. We learnt the ins and outs of the business. We hired experts with vast publishing experience and the passion to do good.

That's how **Global Influencers Publishing House** came to be! Our purpose was clear – to help inspiring leaders and everyday people to share their message with the world, become global thought leaders and empower their readers. We weren't going just to publish books. We were going to create heroes and success stories.

In July 2021, we published our first book, ***#MyVoice***. Within a month, it became an Amazon No.1 Bestseller. Initially we were so busy with the first book, we didn't even think about the next one. But by now we already had so many women wanting to write for the second volume. The funny thing is we didn't even know we would have another volume!

Fast forward one year, by July 2022, we had five volumes of ***#MyVoice*** books, several solo-authored books, each becoming Amazon No.1 Bestsellers and celebrated over 100 bestseller women authors. We completed 36 sessions of the ***#MyVoice*** events and continue to support women through monthly events. In addition, we have presented a unique opportunity to nearly 100 internationally renowned women speakers to share their wisdom and life learnings through our annual ***#MyVoice*** Global Summits, with the next one coming up in October 2022.

We had accomplished our goal of giving a voice to 1000s of women from all over the world, the unsung heroes and community champions, by sharing their inspiring and heart-warming stories with the world. We recognised women who had gone above and beyond the course of work, service, and passions, providing extraordinary examples of courage, resilience, triumph, kindness, compassion, self-love, transformation and success.

Our simple yet powerful initiative is making a difference in the lives of our readers, who often find themselves in the same situation as our authors and can make a lasting change in their own lives—ultimately shifting from living ordinary lives to being extraordinary achievers.

Through our books, we also touch the lives of those in need. We pledged all sales proceeds from the ***#MyVoice*** books to be donated to Singapore Children's Society which is committed to protecting and nurturing children and youth of all races and religions.

The journey is far from over, in fact this is just the beginning for us!

The Lessons Learned

Whilst the pandemic has created havoc worldwide, it has also allowed humanity to slow down, step back and think about what we want from life. It has taught us an important life lesson to be able to pivot and seek alternatives.

In this journey, we also learned that we don't need to look far for inspiration and encouragement but rather learn from people around us who have proved that we all have the power to transform our journeys and create a lasting impact.

My message to anyone reading this chapter is that life will continue to throw at us, both challenges and opportunities. But when we take action, we can turn those challenges into inspiration and make a difference, not just in our life but also in the lives of others. So don't wait for things to happen to you, rather make things happen for you.

"Stories have the power to inspire people to transform their journeys from the ordinary to extraordinary and enable change."

About The Author

Dr. Neera Gupta is an Entrepreneur, Event Organiser, Bestseller Author, TV host, Emcee, Champion Networker, Marketing Guru, Women Empowerment Ambassador, Charity worker........the list goes on. Fun fact: She is also a dentist!

As the Founder & Chief Visionary Officer of Global Influencers, Neera is living her goal of empowering and giving a voice to 1000s of women across the world through the #MyVoice initiative that she started in the midst of pandemic in June 2020. Providing a platform for women to come together to talk about and share their issues and challenges with an aim to become better versions of themselves by listening, learning, helping, and supporting one another through this journey.

Most recently she celebrated the creation of more than 100 Bestseller Women authors in less than one year through the internationally acclaimed #MyVoice book series featuring empowering & inspirational stories of amazing & courageous women, journeying from the ordinary to the extraordinary.

You can connect with Neera at:

Email: *neera@globalinfluencers.sg*

LinkedIn: *linkedin.com/in/drneeragupta*

Facebook: *www.facebook.com/globalinfluencerspublishing*

Raising Your Voice

We all have an opinion, a view or simply, thoughts about things that happen to or around us. Some think, some speak, but the majority do nothing.

But what if you are the one who does something about it and takes charge of a situation, turning challenges into inspiration? Don't you want to be heard and even help those who don't dare to speak? Well, we want to hear from you!

At **GLOBAL INFLUENCERS PUBLISHING HOUSE**, we publish books that inspire, motivate, empower, teach, enrich, connect, inform, stimulate or simply make you laugh.

OUR OBJECTIVE is to connect the hearts and minds of our international readers and authors through the power of words. **THE TEAM** who work behind the scenes, around the clock, making all this magic happen, have been handpicked for their skill, talent, dedication and passion for achieving our objective.

So, if you have a **STORY** to share, send us a message on: **shikha@globalinfluencers.sg**

You can also join the **#MYVOICE FORUM**, which provides a network for like-minded women worldwide to come together to talk about things that matter. A safe space where we can agree, disagree, or agree to disagree but without any judgement, discuss issues and challenges faced, lend a listening ear or a helping hand to one another, find solutions and ultimately take action to make change happen.

To find out more, go to: **www.facebook.com/groups/myvoiceforum**

"Together we will embark on a new journey by creating the world we deserve to live in."

—Neera Gupta,

Chief Visionary Officer at
Global Influencers Publishing House.

Printed in Great Britain
by Amazon